P9-DTA-077

# How—to Grow
# World Class
# Giant
# Pumpkins

*Written by: Don Langevin*

## First Edition

Annedawn Publishing
P.O. Box 247, Norton, MA 02766

# How–to Grow
# World Class
# Giant
# Pumpkins

*Written by: Don Langevin*

Annedawn Publishing

P.O. Box 247–B, Norton, MA 02766

All rights reserved. No part of this book may be reproduced or transmitted in any form or by any means, electronic or mechanical, including photocopying, recording or by any information storage and retrieval system without the written consent of the author, except for inclusion of brief quotations in a review.

Copyright 1993 by Donald G. Langevin
First Printing 1993
Printed in the United States of America
Library of Congress Cataloging in Publication Data
Langevin, Donald G.
How–to Grow World Class Giant Pumpkins / by Don Langevin
1st edition.
Library of Congress Catalog Card Number 93-071941

ISBN 0-9632793-4-3

**All you need is
good seed, good soil,
good weather and good luck!**
Gordon Thomson

# Table of Contents

Chapter 1 What is a Pumpkin?                    1

Chapter 2 The Quest                             7

Chapter 3 The Heavy Hitters                     11

Chapter 4 Securing the Right Seed               47

Chapter 5 Choosing the Growing Area             51

Chapter 6 Preparing the Soil                    53

Chapter 7 Seed Starting                         60

Chapter 8 Planting and Spacing                  65

Chapter 9 Pumpkin Growth Stages                 67

Chapter 10 Plant Protection                     71

Chapter 11 Fertilizing and Watering     76

Chapter 12 Insect and Disease Protection     81

Chapter 13 Weed and Grass Control     91

Chapter 14 Varmint Control     93

Chapter 15 Pollination and Fruit Setting     96

Chapter 16 Pinching and Pruning     101

Chapter 17 Pumpkin Protection     105

Chapter 18 Measuring for Approximate Weight     109

Chapter 19 Competing with Your Pumpkin     111

Appendix     116

## Photographs

There are more than 200 photographs in this book gathered from many, many giant pumpkin growers. These pictures represent the very best images they have of themselves, their pumpkins or their competitive accomplishments. In most cases, these photographs were taken by themselves, friends and family or on occassion, a professional photographer representing the local media. The following people contributed photographs for use in this book, and I offer my apologies to those people not listed here who may have actually taken the pictures:

Howard Dill, Gary Keyzer, Ray Waterman, Hugh Wiberg, George Brooks, Alan Nesbitt, Len Stellpflug, Jerry McGowan, Bill Behuniak, Glen Brown, Pete Glasier, Tom Norlin, Wayne Hackney, Milt Barber, Mark Woodward, Don Fleming, Don Black, Joel Holland, Mike MacDonald, Al Eaton, Fred McDonald, Petoseed, Dr. W. Jarvis, Dr. Doug Gubler, Dr. Benny Bruton, Dr. John Hartman, Dr. Rosie Provvidenti, Sy and Cynthia Chaponis, Gerry Griffin, the WPC and Don Langevin.

Book cover shows Wayne Hackney and his son of New Milford, Connecticut with a championship pumpkin grown in the 1980's.

*Left: George Brook's Granddaughter from North Tewksbury, Ma enjoys pumpkins of all sizes, and the joy is plain to see.*

## About the Author

Don Langevin has worked in the lawn and garden business for over 20 years and his love for growing is only matched by his enthusiasm for writing on various horticultural subjects. He is a graduate of the University of Massachusetts and holds a BBA in Marketing.

His most recent book, *The Growing and Marketing of Fall Mums*, was published in October 1992 and is available from Annedawn Publishing, P.O. Box 247, Norton, MA 02766.

Don has not been growing giant pumpkins for very long, but what he lacks in growing experience is more than compensated by his willingness to go to any length to learn from the top giant pumpkin growers. In compiling data and researching materials, Don contacted all of the top growers and continued to correspond with them right up until press time for this book.

He is a member of both the WPC (World Pumpkin Confederation) and the NEPGA (New England Pumpkin Growers Association) and competes at the Topsfield Fair in Topsfield, Massachusetts.

Don lives with his wife, Anne, and three children in Norton, MA.

## Acknowledgements

It is almost impossible to list all of the people who helped with this book. Growers from all over the United States and Canada contributed photographs and old newsletters from various pumpkin grower organizations. In addition, many people helped with the production of the book—most notably the fine people of Foremost Printers in Providence, Rhode Island.

I would like to thank all of these people and organizations for their help and support during the writing and printing of this book including:

David Reed, Ralph Ferrigno, Richard Simmons, Laura Hurley, Leon Lincoln, Susan Loughlin, Bud Moran, Vernice Kelly, Howard Dill, Don Fleming, Ray Waterman, Pete Glasier, Glen Brown, Tom Norlin, Bill Behuniak, Sy and Cynthia Chaponis, Wayne Hackney, Milt Barber, Mark Woodward, Alan Nesbitt, Hugh Wiberg, Jerry McGowan, Donald Black, Joel Holland, Gary Keyzer, Leonard Stellpflug, Gordon Thomson, Al Eaton, Norm Gallagher, Fred McDonald, Mike MacDonald, George Brooks, Tom Cone, Jon Watterson, Petoseed, the World Pumpkin Confederation, the New England Pumpkin Growers Association, the Midwestern Pumpkin Growers Association, P&P Seed Co., Howard Dill Enterprises and Semline, Inc.

Welcome to the World of World-Class, Giant Pumpkin Growing. If you have never grown a giant pumpkin, rest assured that growing one can be accomplished if you follow some very basic practices. We will cover all of these practices in *How-to-Grow World Class Giant Pumpkins*.

I must warn you though, pumpkin growing enthusiasts are a rather strange, but genuinely, congenial group. To use a cliche borrowed from Will Rogers, "I have never met a pumpkin grower that I didn't like."

You will not experience the true meaning of this last paragraph until you bring a pumpkin to a regional weighoff or join one of the pumpkin growing organizations. The comradeship among pumpkin growers is real and unrestrained. You will make many new friends, and learn new ways to give and receive friendship.

Selfishness is rarely encountered among pumpkin growers. They will give you seed, secrets and friendship just because you are a pumpkin grower, and they will give you limitless encouragement to grow pumpkins that even exceed their own in size.

*Gary Keyzer and Kids, Nekoosa, Wisconsin*

There are thousands of pumpkin growers in the U.S., Canada, and elsewhere in the world, who belong to pumpkin growing organizations. Their numbers have been steadily growing for 10 years, and recently their ranks have begun to swell as they pursue, with anticipation a feat thought to be impossible only 5–10 years ago.

Yes, the quest for the 1000-Pound Pumpkin has captivated pumpkin growers around the world. Since 1987, Ray Waterman, president of the World Pumpkin Confederation has sounded the drum beat for nothing short of the goal of the 1000-pound pumpkin. Ask any serious pumpkin grower. Each has his own dream that this year's pumpkin will yield yet another world record or the ultimate goal of a 1000-Pound Dill's Atlantic Giant.

Because this group is so unselfish, this is not idle or ill-conceived dreaming. The very best of seed is always shared and new cultural information is freely conveyed through the various organizational newsletters. Thus, anyone with the right knowledge and guidance can grow a truly giant pumpkin.

I hope that this book allows you the opportunity to grow a large pumpkin, but most of all, I hope this book encourages you to experience the people of World-Class Giant Pumpkin Growing.

*Above: Teamwork and ingenuity are the hallmarks of competitive pumpkin growers. Here, six men move a 600-pound pumpkin from the pumpkin patch to a waiting pickup truck.*
*Right: Squash are green, pumpkins are orange. There are many thousands of giant squash growers who compete alongside pumpkin growers at annual weigh-offs.*

*George Brook's granddaughter poses next to a 607-pound Jack O'Lantern which won the New England Championship in 1991*

# Chapter One What is a Pumpkin?

Ask ten different pumpkin growers what a pumpkin is and you are likely to get ten different (and probably right) answers. Some of these answers will be scientifically based while others will be based on visual characteristics, but the one constant among all these growers is that none is really confident that their answer is entirely correct. This is not to say that pumpkin growers are not knowledgeable about their crop. Competitive pumpkin growers are very bright, very committed, and personally, some of the finest people you will ever meet. The confusion and uncertainty about pumpkins is partly caused from its relationship to squash and gourds, and the incredible amount of folklore that has been passed down for hundreds of years.

## Squash are Green, Pumpkins are Orange

The official rules of the World Pumpkin Confederation(WPC) state that to be considered a pumpkin, the fruit must be 80% orange to yellow. From here, all else is questionable. The confusion starts, perhaps, when we try to define a pumpkin. Look in any encyclopedia, good horticultural reference or dictionary and you are liable to receive directions to go elsewhere for your answer.

The *Webster's New Collegiate Dictionary* defines pumpkins as:

> *1a: the usually round deep yellow fruit of a vine (Cucurbita pepo) of the gourd family widely cultivated as food. b: Winter Crookneck. c: any of various large-fruited winter squashes (Cucurbita maxima). 2: a usually hairy, prickly vine that produces pumpkins.*

From these definitions, can you really determine what a pumpkin is? Is it Cucurbita pepo, a Winter Crookneck or a winter squash (C. maxima)?

In *The Pumpkin King* by Al Kingsbury, the author states,

> *"The giant pumpkin family (genus Cucurbita C. maxima) contains a large assortment of plant characteristics which offer possibility of new combinations of bigger and better pumpkins."*

Look up pumpkins in *Wyman's Gardening Encyclopedia* (regarded as one of the most complete, definitive and accurate horticultural references in print) and you will find the direction,

> *"See Squash."*

Top: *Alan Nesbitt prepares to trim a giant squash.*
Bottom: *Len Stellpflug with an Atlantic Giant Pumpkin.*

Wyman goes on to say, under the heading of Squash and Pumpkins that,

*"These two crops are grouped together because their culture is similar and also because of the confusion in nomenclature."*

Even the most brilliant horticulturists have reservations over their definition of pumpkins.

The only real agreement among growers, plant scientists and horticulturists is that pumpkins belong to the genus: Cucurbita. This genus is a member of the Cucumber Family (Cucurbitaceae) and includes all of the vine crops defined as cucumbers, melons, summer and winter squash, gourds and pumpkins. Cucumbers and melons belong to an entirely different genus (Cucumis) and plant scientists place their origins in Asia and Africa. As such, they do not enter into the equation which defines what a pumpkin really is. A pumpkin is not a cucumber or a melon.

Of the Cucurbita genus, three species boast pumpkins as members (C. pepo. C. moschata and C. maxima). Each species has popular and common varietal members. C. pepo has the Connecticut Field and Small Sugar Pumpkin, C. moschata has Large Cheese and C. maxima boasts the Dill's Atlantic Giant. This book probably would not be written, or the sport of pumpkin growing as far advanced if it were not for the Dill's Atlantic Giant. With no disrespect intended, Dill's Atlantic Giant will be referred to many times in this book as merely the Atlantic Giant, which is the "lingo" of most of today's competitive growers. Developed and patented by Howard Dill of Nova Scotia, Canada, the seed from the Atlantic Giant has been used, almost exclusively, for the last 8-10 years by anyone seriously raising world-class, giant pumpkins. The sport of giant pumpkin growing may not owe its origin to Howard Dill, but the advancement of the sport would not have been possible without his persistent inbreeding of the Atlantic Giant. It can be definitely stated that the Atlantic Giant is a member of the species C. maxima.

For lack of a better name, some people call any large pumpkin or squash a "squmpkin". This name was coined by Hugh Wiberg in 1971 when an accidental cross between a Hungarian Squash and a Big Max Pumpkin produced an offspring weighing 280 pounds. Wiberg's display of this particular offspring at the Topsfield Fair in Topsfield, Massachusetts, and his free distribution of "squmpkin" seeds throughout the mid to late 1970's to thousands of New England gardeners, helped to create an awareness of cucurbits that may very well have gone undiscovered for many years. Wiberg is the director of the New England Pumpkin Growers Association (NEPGA).

Pumpkins come in all sizes and shapes. They are used for ornamental and decorative use, as well as being consumed as food. They can range in size from a few ounces to 827 pounds (the World Record held by Joel Holland of Puyallup, WA set in 1992). The variety choice is almost endless with many individual varieties receiving much attention because of their uniformity in size, shape or color, and their consistency in serving the needs of various commercial and residential users. Howard Dill's seed cata-

*Pumpkins come in many sizes and shapes. The varieties on these pages serve the needs of their growers very well*
*Top: Spirit*
*Middle: Jack O'Lantern*
*Bottom: Dill's Atlantic Giant*

*Top: Ghost Rider*
*Middle: Howden*
*Bottom: Jack-Be-Little*

log features six varieties earmarked for specific use or markets. Even the man who developed the famed Dill's Atlantic Giant, the largest of all pumpkins, sees the benefits of growing smaller, more commercial varieties.

Commercial pumpkin growers need varieties that will serve the needs of their customers. Varieties like "Jack-Be-Little", one of the world's smallest pumpkins, is highly sought for its use in Fall decorating on a miniature scale. Growing only a few inches in diameter, Jack-Be-Little's are seen almost everywhere you look in the fall — from restaurant tables to win-dowsills to car dashboards. Another variety, "Howden," developed from the famous Connecticut Field Pumpkin, is grown for its uniform size which serves the needs of pumpkin lovers who want large pumpkins ranging in weight from 25-40 pounds. It is a great variety for door-step decorating or carving. "Jack O'Lantern" is a very popular variety that was developed for the home owner looking for a small, carving pumpkin. Shape, size and extraordinary color combine to make it one of the most appealing choices of fall pumpkins. Of course, the "Dill's Atlantic Giant" is sought by all competitive pumpkin growers and homeowners wanting large, exhibition size pumpkins. Although other large varieties like Burpee's "Prizewinner" have better color, and the "Big Max" have more uniform shape, none com-mands the appeal of the Atlantic Giant when it calls for all-out size.

## Common Characteristics of All Pumpkins

There are some characteristics which are common to all pumpkins, and knowing them will help you to understand what a pumpkin really is. All pumpkins are annuals, and are extremely frost tender. This means that a pumpkin completes its life cycle of growth in a single growing season. Seed which germinates and grows through the summer will produce seed in the Fall which will carry on the annual cycle of life the following spring. Seedlings which germinate prematurely, or seedlings not protected from sub-freezing temperatures will perish. The growing season for pumpkins, therefore, starts when frost-free days have been reached. For each of us, this date may be slightly different. It takes between 120–150 days to grow a large pumpkin. Although there are varieties that mature in less time, they do not size-up as well as the Dill's Atlantic Giant, Prizewinner or Big Max.

All pumpkins are summer growers meaning that their optimum growth spurt occurs during the warmest time of the year. George Brooks, a very competitive large pumpkin grower from North Tewksbury, Massachusetts has documented giant pumpkin growth for years, and has observed this char-acteristic in many pumpkins. Most pumpkin growers believe that the 4th of July is the beginning of the growth spurt period, and only declining average daily low temperatures and diminishing sunlight brings an end to it.

All pumpkins are vine crops and their vines contain tendrils which fasten to anything which is available for the purpose of anchoring the plant. Tendrils are Mother Nature's way of protecting vine crops. Pumpkins have very large leaves dispersed on vines over very large areas. These leaves are constantly battered by wind, hail and rain throughout the season. Tendrils and anchor roots occurring along the vines help to reduce movement, and as such, protects the plant from wind and other forces. Competitive pumpkin growers are keenly aware of this protective device and many of them try to enhance the benefits from anchored vines by constructing wind screens to reduce the forces of nature and by anchoring the vine using various methods discussed later in this book.

*Left: Tendrils are a distinguishing trait of all pumpkin plants.*
*Below: "Elephant-Ear" leaves can measure more than 2 feet across.*

Most all pumpkin varieties have vines which have prickly-hairy coverings. These coverings can range from moderately sticky to, sometimes, razor sharpness. This covering feels much like Velcro™ and works much the same. Small insects are occasionally snared or injured while some predators are sometimes discouraged from roaming amongst the patch. This is yet another characteristic of the pumpkin which has evolved to help it remain a robust grower.

All pumpkins have separate male and female flowers occurring on the same plant. Pollination, the movement of pollen from the male flower to the female flower parts, is generally carried out by bees seeking nectar from the flowers. Selective hand pollination is carried out by most competitive pumpkin growers to insure better and more controllable pollination.

It is commonly believed that pumpkins will cross with any vine crop, but this is not true. In fact, they rarely cross-pollinate with other plants outside their species, and never cross with other genus. The folklore that suggests that pumpkins cross with cucumbers, zucchini squash or watermelons is a good example. The Atlantic Giant, which is a member of the species maxima, will only cross-pollinate with some varieties within this species, and in a limited way with some of the yellow-flowered gourds of the species C. pepo ovifera (Turk's Caps). If you are growing pumpkins to obtain seed which has reliable characteristics in its offspring, then selective pollination and protection along with plant isolation will be necessary. In this way, no new characteristics enter the "gene bank" that carries the characteristics of the plant to the following year's progeny. Most of us will never get this far, choosing to grow only the very best seed we can obtain each year from people who have developed consistent, outstanding characteristics in their plants.

Pumpkins have hard outer walls, and like all Winter Squash, are not eaten when they are young or not fully matured. This is dramatically different than the Summer Squash which are eaten only when their outer walls are thin and tender, and discarded when they begin to thicken and harden. Pumpkins have enjoyed hundreds of years of use as food for both man and animals. The pumpkin's association with Thanksgiving gives us evidence that it was an important food to early settlers in America, and grown by Native Americans for hundreds of years before. Pumpkins have their ori-

*Above: The hallmark of any large, durable giant pumpkin is its thick walls which support its tremendous weight.*
*Right: A Coke can gives scale to the thickness of a Dill's Atlantic Giant's outer walls.*
*Below: Bill Behuniak's yard is taken over by a giant pumpkin plant. It is not unusual for plants to cover 1000-2000 square feet.*

gins in the New World. This observation serves to further the distinction between pumpkins and other vine crops like cucumbers and melons which originated in Asia and Africa.

All pumpkins are robust, aggressive growers capable of covering ground very quickly. Even the smallest bush types can have vines 8–10 feet long. An average pumpkin patch will cover an area 20' x 20' (400 square feet), although most varieties easily exceed these measurements with giant pumpkins covering anywhere from 800–1200 square feet. This fast growth com-

bined with characteristically large "elephant ear" leaves serves to create a canopy over the growing area. This results in cooler soil temperatures, due to the shade created by the leaf covering, and less competition from rival annual and perennial weeds and grasses.

Pumpkins are yellow to orange with some notably orange/red. Most competitive pumpkin growers use this as the only gauge for distinguishing pumpkins from squash. When you take a large fruit to a regional weighoff site in the Fall, your category of competition will be determined by the fruit's color. If it is green or gray, it will be determined to be a squash, and if it is yellow or orange it will qualify as a pumpkin. Most regional weighoff sites have competitions for both pumpkins and squash, but remember, the real show stoppers are the giant pumpkins. Never fear if your desire is to grow giant squash as opposed to growing giant pumpkins. There are some very good giant squash varieties to grow. One variety, named Collins, has produced many world record weights. Some of these weights have rivaled the weight of the Atlantic Giant Pumpkin. Len Stellpflug of Rush, NY, a world record grower of giant squash, has grown two giant squash over 800 pounds (807 and 821). His 821 pound monster is only 6 pounds shy of the weight of the largest pumpkin ever grown. Len vows that someday he will break the world record for the largest pumpkin as well. So, no matter what you decide to grow, pumpkins or squash, there will be people out there to compete with, and challenges each and every season.

If you buy good seed from reputable growers which have been approved by Howard Dill, the choice of category, squash or pumpkins, will be easily predicted from year to year. If you decide to grow your own seed, and you are not careful of pollination techniques and isolation from other members of the species C. maxima, your seed offspring could bring you some unpleasant surprises. What you thought was a pumpkin, could very well be judged as a squash.

Remember that squash are green and pumpkins are orange.

*Howard Dill shows-off his niece and a Dill's Atlantic Giant Pumpkin in 1983. The seed from this pumpkin produced the world's first 500 and 600-pound pumpkins.*

*Howard Dill and his grandson, Alex.*

# Chapter 2 The Quest

There are few things which motivate men more than breaking barriers which other men thought were impossible. Breaking world speed records, running the first sub-4-minute mile, climbing Mount Everest or diving miles below the ocean's surface have all captivated mans' attention, but there are many lesser known world records that have also influenced men. In fact, any world record category seems to elicit responses from man which could never be anticipated. *The Guinness Book of World Records* is crammed with them and *Ripley's Believe It or Not* has chronicled some of the more bazaar of these preoccupations for many decades. Add to this the fact that a major obstacle or barrier is within sight, and you have all the makings for a full scale assault by intensely committed people.

This, by definition, is a quest. The Webster's New Collegiate Dictionary calls it,

*"A search, pursuit or investigation."*

Most quests combine the efforts of many men to reach a goal thought to be impossible. The quest for the Holy Grail by Sir Richard the Lion Hearted, which many imagine when hearing the word quest, captivated millions of men and changed the face of history forever. The quest for the first 1000-pound pumpkin began in earnest only after the Atlantic Giant Pumpkin seed was introduced in the 1980's. In less than 15 years, the momentum in breaking world records has accelerated and the appearance of new faces among the die-hard, veteran growers has escalated. At last count there were about 2 million gardeners around the world growing the Atlantic Giant, and many thousands of them belong to grower organizations which hold annual festivals and weigh-offs. This formidable group will indeed continue to swell as more and more people are pulled along in the quest for the first 1000 pounder.

There is much confidence that the first 1000-pound pumpkin will be grown sometime within the next 5–10 years. This confidence has lured the average, backyard gardener into the quest and brought tremendous attention to the sport of giant pumpkin growing.

There is also much to gain from growing the first 1000 pound pumpkin. The first grower who succeeds will become instantly famous in the ranks of competitive pumpkin growers and may very well become a celebrity in his region of the country. His name will not only go into the record books, it will become part of history. This simple fact will live forever in the minds of men who chronicle records, just as Babe Ruth's 60 home runs in 1927 lives in the mind of every youngster that has ever picked up a baseball bat. There will be countless interviews by journalists and talk show hosts, and a

*Three up-and-coming giant pumpkin growers, and good friends, left to right: Tony Ciliberto of Wilkes-Barre, PA, Gerry Griffin, of Amston, CT, and Alan Nesbitt, of Conesus, NY.*

bevy of product endorsement proposals from many horticultural industry companies, and the first to reach 1000 pounds will be crowned the undisputed world champion and the new Pumpkin King.

So, there will be fame and fortune also involved in the quest. Nothing motivates man more than the lure of either of these yet, pumpkin growing will still be a leisure time activity for the millions of people who garden and grow pumpkins just for the fun of it and for the Jack O'Lanterns they produce for Halloween.

Since 1978, only 15 years ago, the records have been smashed on average every 3 years, with current history seeing a new world record about every other year. The average increase in world record pumpkins since 1978 has been about 25 pounds per year. Since 1984 it has averaged about 37 pounds and, more recently, from 1989 to 1992, the average yearly increase in word record pumpkins has been over 39 pounds. You can see now why there is much anticipation that the 1000-pound pumpkin is not very far off in the future. In fact, it has only been in the last few years that people have actually voiced an opinion that it was even possible. Before that, it was mostly idle dreaming. The current world record, held by Joel Holland of Puyallup, Washington was achieved in 1992 with an 827-pound Atlantic Giant. If we do a little mathematical forecasting, we could see a world record, 1000-pound pumpkin grown in 1997, and I think, earlier if more people join in on the quest.

There is always the chance that weights will become stymied at the 800 pound level, much the same as they were in the early 1900's at 400 pounds, but I think not. Where world records were the only motivating force in years past, the all consuming quest now seems to be nothing short of 1000 pounds. Competitive pumpkin growing ranks will swell, like boom times in a gold rush, in anticipation of striking the mother lode and growing the first 1000 pounder. All will have that same dream of becoming part of history and the next Pumpkin King.

*Right: Howard Dill with his 1981 world record pumpkin. This 493.5-pounder held the world record for 4 years while Howard won an unprecedented 4 consecutive World Championships.*

# Chapter 3 The Heavy Hitters

The Heavy Hitters in the world of giant pumpkin growing come from all parts of the world and all walks of life. No one profession or stage of life seems to immune people bitten by the desire to raise a giant pumpkin. Some are commercial growers, but the lion's share of them are just backyard gardeners whose joy for growing evolved from tending vegetables in a small plot for their families.

What distinguishes the Heavy Hitters from ordinary giant pumpkin growers is the contribution they have made to the sport. World records and world championships certainly qualify, but other significant achievements also determine who is called a Heavy Hitter. In developing the list for this book, I considered the weight of pumpkins grown, along with consistency from year to year, and contributions to the research and development side as well as the organizational side of the sport. Of course, no one stands out more obviously than Howard Dill. Whole books have been written about Howard, and hundreds of articles and stories have appeared in newspapers and magazines throughout Canada, the United States and around the World. A true gentleman with time for any grower, Howard has achieved a folklore-like image. It seems that every competitive pumpkin grower has a story to tell about Howard with each of them revolving somehow around his casual, down-to-earth manner, and his kind and gentle way. It is only fitting that we start this chapter on The Heavy Hitters with The Pumpkin King, Howard Dill.

*Left: Howard Dill with a world record Dill's Atlantic Giant Pumpkin.*
*Right: Howard's Mailbox receives more than 5000 letters and seed orders each year at his home in Windsor, Nova Scotia, Canada.*

## Howard Dill

Peter and Nancy Rigoloso of Bremerton, WA said in a foreword to the book, *The Pumpkin King*,

> *"Howard Dill is singularly the most important person*
> *in the world of championship pumpkin growing."*

Howard's accomplishments, as well as his years of service to all pumpkin growers is testimony to these words. No other person is more deserving of the title of The Pumpkin King.

Howard was born and raised on a small farm on College Road in Windsor, Nova Scotia, Canada that has been in the Dill family since the 1800's. Pumpkin growing has somehow been a part of his life for as long as he can remember. Howard began growing pumpkins with his father William "Dick" Dill at an early age and built on that experience and the experiences of many championship growers before him. As a young man, his interest in pumpkin growing matured into pumpkin breeding, and each year he would observe what he and his father had grown, always looking for traits that might be valuable in increasing the weight of a pumpkin. As Howard says,

> *"After examining the characteristics of several pumpkins,*
> *I noticed likes and dislikes that I would set my sights on*
> *in my quest to develop a much larger pumpkin."*

In 1967, Howard broke the 100 pound barrier and by 1969 was growing 200 pounders. Although this was considered huge for his day and region, the world record was an amazing 403 pounds set by William Warnock of Goderich, Ontario, Canada in 1903 and displayed at the World's Fair in St. Louis, Missouri that same year. That record would stand for 75 years.

William Warnock had written directions for growing giant pumpkins, and Howard read them eagerly. Another interesting link between Howard and William Warnock exists in the seed that each planted. Howard's father had been growing pumpkins for many years with seed purchased from the

*Top: Joshua Dill seems a little bewildered at the size of his uncle's giant pumpkin. Howard's 1981 specimen broke the world record at 493.5 pounds.*
*Below: Howard seems a little embarrassed by all of the attention but very proud of his achievements.*
*Left: A striking display of "Dill Boulders" that could mesmerize even the most complacent non-gardener.*

*Top: Hilda Dill devilishly smiles from the inside of Howard's first world record pumpkin. This pumpkin put Howard in Ripley's Believe It Or Not.*
*Right: Howard Dill's mailbox at the mouth of the farm driveway.*
*Bottom: Howard examines an early-set fruit.*

Rennie Seed Company in Ontario. Although they are out of business now, the importance of their existence, as it relates to modern giant pumpkin growing, was their purchase of William Warnock's World Record Pumpkin of 1903 and the subsequent sale of its seed to farmers all over Canada. They purchased the pumpkin for a mere $10 and sold the seed for 25 cents each, under the name of Goderich Giant (the home of Warnock).

Howard began cross-pollinating the Goderich Giant with another variety his father had been growing for over 30 years called, Genuine Mammoth. Howard grew both for many years, selectively hand-pollinating each variety until in 1973 he claims to have finally isolated the two strains. These two strains would form the parental backbone of the now famous Dill's Atlantic Giant Pumpkin. Howard grew both strains for a number of years, experimenting with cross-pollination of the two until he had isolated certain characteristics that he considered favorable. In 1977, this new strain seemed quite stable in passing its genes and characteristics along to its seed offspring, and by the early 1980's, he began the long process of plant patent application for the Dill's Atlantic Giant.

In 1979 Howard broke the 75-year-old record of William Warnock with a 438.5 pound pumpkin weighed at the Cornell Pumpkin Show in Philadelphia, Pennsylvania and was featured in *Ripley's Believe It or Not*. From 1979 through 1984, Howard was unbeatable in the world of championship pumpkin growing, and his 493.5 pounder in 1981 earned him distinction in the *Guinness Book of World Records*. And so, the torch of William Warnock was passed to the new Pumpkin King, Howard Dill.

Howard missed winning a 5th consecutive world championship in 1983 by a mere 5 pounds.

In 1983 Howard cofounded, with Ray Waterman of Collins, New York, the World Pumpkin Confederation (WPC), which has developed a network of weighoff sites to track each year's pumpkin weights and supply information to over 2000 members throughout the world.

In 1991 Howard was jointly inducted into the WPC Pumpkin Growers Hall of Fame and awarded the Lifetime Achievement and Service Award. No doubt, these two awards will never be given simultaneously again to any other grower of pumpkins. It is only fitting that Howard have this distinct honor.

Howard's importance stretches far beyond his achievements. For not only is he a world champion, world record holder and cofounder of the WPC, he is also a tender, gentle and giving man. Many growers have gotten their start from Howard with seed, advice and encouragement. Just about anyone, even today after all the fame and notoriety, can pick up the phone, dial his phone number and find Howard on the other end, ready to answer your questions.

If you would like to learn more about Howard, order seed directly from him or purchase his book, *The Pumpkin King* write to: Howard Dill, 400 College Road, Windsor, Nova Scotia, Canada BON 2TO.

*Top: Howard winning another blue ribbon and a 4th consecutive World Championship in 1982.*
*Below: Howard receives the Lifetime Achievement Award from the WPC in 1991 and is simultaneously inducted into the WPC Giant Pumpkin Growers Hall of Fame.*
*Left: Anxious moments as Howard awaits an official weight.*

## Ray Waterman

Few people are better known in the world of giant pumpkin growing than Howard Dill or Ray Waterman. Ray has been a serious grower of world class giant vegetables for many years, and with Howard Dill, co-founded the World Pumpkin Confederation in 1983. It is perhaps Ray's visions about the sport of growing giant vegetables and his organizational abilities which sets him apart from all other pumpkin growers.

The son of a chicken farmer, Ray inherited his father's drive and determination, and the WPC has flourished because of his leadership. Boasting over 2000 members, the WPC, with its newsletters to members, has formed the backbone of a body of people dedicated to the sport of giant pumpkin growing. As this body of people increases in the upcoming years because of the quest for the first 1000 pound pumpkin, it will have Ray Waterman to thank for enabling it to happen.

*Top: Ray Waterman and Ayo Ogungbuyi behind the third largest pumpkin ever grown 780.5 pounds and officially weighed at the 1991 WPC Championship in Collins, NY.*
*Right: Ray outside the family restaurant in Collins, NY.*
*Below: Ray with his amazing, 99" world record long gourd.*

Ray is a successful restaurant owner in Collins, New York who still finds the time to plant and maintain 22 acres of vegetables. 12 acres of these 22 are planted to Jack O'Lantern pumpkins for Fall sales, but 10 acres are planted to giant vegetables. Ray grows giant tomatoes, cabbage, kohlrabi, long and broad beans, cucumbers, long gourds, corn, radish, sunflower and just about any vegetable that anyone attempts to compete with. Ray sells seeds from these giant vegetables to growers all over the world, and his seed company, P & P Seed Co. also sells reliable, certified Dill's Atlantic Giant seed. He holds the world record for the longest gourd ever grown (99 inches), and he ranks third all time with a 780.5 pound pumpkin he grew in 1991 with Ayo Ogungbuyi. Ray's family also competes. His sister, Karen Fisher grew a 742 pound pumpkin in 1991 and his brother Paul a 658.5 pounder in 1990. These pumpkins all reside in the top 30 largest pumpkins ever grown.

But, if Ray Waterman had never grown a world class pumpkin, he would still be included in this book because of the contributions he has made to the sport. He has almost single-handedly made Collins, New York the center of the universe for competitive pumpkin growers. Ray organizes and synchronizes the weighoff of pumpkins for the WPC, so that by weighoff day's end, an official accounting of pumpkins from all over the World is established.

*Above: Ray and Ayo Ogungbuyi behind a mammoth Dill's Atlantic Giant Pumpkin.*

*Left: Ray's twin brothers, Peter and Paul Waterman are accomplished pumpkin growers as well. This picture shows them in 1983 with the largest pumpkin ever grown in the United States, up to that time, at 465 pounds.*

*Below: A young Ray Waterman and a winning pumpkin.*

It was Ray's dream to create an "Olympics" for vegetable growing which would provide a forum of competition where growers and the love of growing vegetables would finally be glorified.

If you would like to write to Ray, join the WPC or buy seed from P & P Seed Co., address your inquiries to World Pumpkin Confederation, 14050 Gowanda State Road, Collins, New York 14034.

## Pete Glasier

Pete Glasier is the kind of man that will talk to anyone on just about any subject for hours and hours. He is not only interesting and articulate, but also fun to listen to. If the subject happens to be giant pumpkins, you will be listening to one of the most knowledgeable growers anywhere in the world. Pete has been growing giant pumpkins since 1981 when he came across a picture of the Atlantic Giant and Howard Dill. He contacted Howard personally by telephone, that's Pete's way, and before long had received seed, advice and a lot of encouragement to plant a giant pumpkin.

Pete considers his most significant contribution to pumpkin growing as being an ambassador for the sport. Pete has personally introduced and encouraged many new growers. He feels that the more people exposed to the sport, the better the chance of new world record achievements.

In 1991, he and his wife Cindi set out on different paths from their Denver, Colorado home. Pete went to The Nut Tree, WPC weigh-off in Vacaville, California and Cindi went to the Half Moon Bay Pumpkin Festival in Half Moon Bay, California. Cindi won at Half Moon Bay with a 602 pounder which attracted so much attention that people from all over the world, and from all walks of life began noticing what competitive pumpkin growers were doing. CNN covered the Half Moon Bay event and Cindi appeared on TV throughout the US and many other parts of the world. Her parents, who were living in Hawaii, even saw her and her pumpkin on TV! Newspapers throughout the US and Canada carried front page stories and pictures of Cindi with her giant.

Pete has traveled to many of the major pumpkin weigh-off sites in North America at one time or another including: Half Moon Bay, California, Vancouver, British Columbia, Collins, New York, Clackamas, Oregon and Windsor, Nova Scotia. In driving from Denver to Half Moon Bay, Pete and Cindi logged an amazing 2500 miles round trip. This alone shows how serious Pete is about the sport.

At 63 years of age, he has been a farmer all of his life until recently retiring and assuming his new job description, "Giant Pumpkin Grower." His dedication to the sport is so intense that he packed up his belongings in Denver, Colorado and moved to Sequim, Washington where he claims the climate and the soil are more suited for growing big pumpkins. You can see that the pursuit of growing giant pumpkins does not diminish with age. If anything, it grows stronger.

The picture on this page shows Pete with his winning entry at the WPC Clackamas, Oregon weigh-off in 1992. That pumpkin weighed 637 pounds and ranks 24th all time. Pete will not stop until everyone is growing giant pumpkins.

If you would like to correspond with Pete, write to: Pete Glasier, 62 Clover Lane, Sequim, Washington 98382

Don't be surprised if he calls you back, no matter where you live!

*Pete Glasier with his winning entry at the WPC Clackamas, Oregon Weighoff. This pumpkin tipped the scales at 637 pounds.*

## Glen Brown

Glen Brown has been growing giant pumpkins only since 1985, but he has already broken into the WPC Top 30 pumpkins of all time twice with a 710 pounder in 1992 and a 699.5 pounder in 1991. This double entry in the elite Top 30 shows just how much Glen knows about growing giant pumpkins. Consistency and the ability to duplicate achievements is the sign of every Heavy Hitter in this sport. Take heart though, Glen's first pumpkin weighed only 220 pounds, and until he started growing Atlantic Giant seeds in 1986, growing pumpkins was only a hobby. Now it's an obsession.

Glen feel that he gets his most satisfying moments not from growing pumpkins, but from seeing the look on people's faces as they look at what he has grown. Glen displays his pumpkins at the Minnesota State Fair and the Anamosa, IA (Ryan Norlin Memorial) pumpkin weigh-off. He never tires of answering questions and helping people get started in the sport.

Glen stresses the need for new growers to seek information from the veterans, build up your soil with compost, manure and other organic materials and get good seed from the top growers. Try several different seed sources each year.

Glen may have been destined to be a giant pumpkin grower. He was born on October 31, 1949 — yes, Halloween! He grew up on a farm as a boy and still works in the horticulture business to this day.

Glen loves to talk about pumpkins and growing giants. If you would like to write to him, simply address your inquiry to: Glen Brown, 5702 229th Avenue, Bethel, Minnesota 55005

*Glen Brown and his daughter, Amber, flank a 710-pound pumpkin which easily won first place at the WPC Ryan Norlin Memorial Pumpkin Weighoff in Anamosa, Iowa in 1992.*

## Tom Norlin

Tom Norlin has never grown a pumpkin which weighed over 382 pounds, and if he never does, it will not prevent him from becoming one of The Heavy Hitters in today's world of competitive pumpkin growing. You see, Tom Norlin's contribution to the sport of pumpkin growing goes beyond personal achievements, and beyond the mere growing of pumpkins. Tom has been growing pumpkins for over 30 years and along the way has introduced many to the sport and provided leadership for growers looking for someone to take the responsibility of planning each year's weigh-off and associated festivities.

In 1989, the first WPC Ryan Norlin Memorial Pumpkin Weigh-off was staged in Anamosa, Iowa, and the number of participants and spectators has been steadily growing ever since. Part of this is because of Tom Norlin and part is because of the vision every competitive pumpkin grower has of the Ryan Norlin tragedy.

Tom Norlin's nine year old nephew, Ryan, was his protege. Growing pumpkins was a team effort and the team of Ryan and Tom was one filled with love for one another and love for the sport of pumpkin growing. In 1989, on a blistering hot summer day on the Mississippi River, Ryan lost his life in a boating accident.

If you pursue the sport of competitive pumpkin growing, you will come to know that growers who share their knowledge and time with you become family regardless of their relationship. If one of your pumpkin growing friends is also a close family member, it will bring the two of you even closer together. This is why so many fathers introduce their children to gardening, and why pumpkin growing will always remain a way to show how much we love one another. Tom Norlin's love for Ryan made possible one of the most popular pumpkin weigh-offs in the world and along the way created a forum for pumpkin growers all over the Midwest.

Ryan Norlin will never be forgotten, nor will the relationship that every pumpkin grower has with someone who has introduced him to the sport.

In 1993 Tom, with the help of Glen Brown and Gary Keyzer, organized the Midwestern Pumpkin Growers Association whose goal it is to catch up to the world class growers and bring home a world record before the 1990's are over.

Tom can be easily approached, as most pumpkin growers are. If you wish, you may write to him by addressing your inquiry to: Tom Norlin, Box 247, Hopkinton, Iowa 52237

*Above: Tom Norlin with his wife Peg, daughter Laura, son Jacob and dog Whiskers prior to leaving for the annual pumpkin weighoff. Below: Ryan Norlin.*

## Wayne Hackney

Wayne Hackney first began growing giant pumpkins in 1983 and produced an amazingly small 73-pound pumpkin that year. Attending the Eastern States Exposition (The Big E) in West Springfield, Massachusetts (one of the largest agricultural fairs in the Northeast) in 1983, Wayne stood in awe of the 250-pound pumpkins of Charles Eastlund who had won the pumpkin growing championship for many years at the fair. Wayne is not an average giant pumpkin grower by any stretch of the imagination, nor is he the average person you will ever meet. He is the kind of person who rolls up his sleeves and really gets into the flow of getting something accomplished — and accomplished right!

In the Winter of 1984, Wayne read a *Wall Street Journal* article about Howard Dill and the Dill's Atlantic Giant. Dill had grown a 493 pound pumpkin in 1981 and was heralded as the world champion. In true fashion, Wayne looked Howard up, struck up a friendship which lasts to this day and came away with some tips and some Atlantic Giant seeds for the 1984 season.

Little did Wayne know at the time, but that Wall Street Journal article, the talk with Dill and the Atlantic Giant seed would lead to a 440-pound pumpkin, the Eastern States Exposition Championship, the Topsfield Fair Pumpkin Weigh-off Championship and the bragging rights to the largest pumpkin ever grown in New England.

This is part and parcel of Wayne Hackney. Nothing really is luck or by chance with him. You may call the coincidence of the Wall Street Journal article and the use of Atlantic Giant seed chance, but anyone that knows Wayne knows that faced with his 73-pound pumpkin of 1983, he would be bound and determined to improve the very next season. Wayne will go to any lengths to improve his chances of growing a larger pumpkin. Along the way he has made friendships and developed associates in every scientific walk of life which even remotely touches on the growing of cucurbits. If anyone publishes an article on any aspect of growing cucurbits, Wayne will be quickly on this trail for personal information as it relates to pumpkin growing. As a result, Wayne is considered one of the most knowledgeable pumpkin growers in the world. Despite his endless fascination with the subject, Wayne still remains a hard working, devoted family man who contributes much of his time to pumpkin growing organizations, the community and his church.

In 1985 Wayne's pumpkin tipped the scales at 515 pounds at The Big E, and still holds the all-time record there. But The Big E is not an official weigh-off site for world championship pumpkins because of its early season dates. Wayne had to wait for the Topsfield Fair in Topsfield, Massachusetts, for an official weigh in. This was 3 weeks later. You will come to learn that pumpkins begin losing weight almost as soon as they are cut from the vine. The loss of water is tremendous, and if a pumpkin develops a soft spot, and begins to rot, the season is over. Wayne's 515-pound pumpkin never made it to Topsfield that year. Instead, the largest pumpkin grown anywhere in the world that year was a 515-pound giant by Scott Cully weighed at the Topsfield Fair. That is as close as anyone will get to winning a world championship without winning. It is "the one that got away" story, but it does show how Wayne the man operates. Most pumpkin growers just want to enjoy growing their pumpkins and an opportunity to get them weighed. Prize money and notoriety are really secondary to them. Wayne is a pumpkin grower who exemplifies these virtues in spite of the fact that he is one of The Heavy Hitters in today's world of competitive pumpkin growing.

Wayne grew a 614-pound pumpkin in 1989 which was the largest pumpkin ever grown in New England up to that time and, it remained the New England record until 1991.

If you would like to write to Wayne, send your letters to: Wayne Hackney, 227 Carmen Hill #2, New Milford, Connecticut 06776.

*Left page:*
> *Top: Wayne congratulates Melissa Malec, his ten-year-old student, on a fine showing at the Eastern States Exposition.*
> *Middle: Wayne with wife, Sue, children and the 1984 "Big E" and Topsfield Fair champion pumpkin.*
> *Bottom: Kate Hackney sits atop the 1989 New England Champion pumpkin at 614-pounds.*

*Right page:*
> *Below: This "Cinderella Coach" was constructed for the 1985 Big E pumpkin show and is shown with a 300-pound specimen.*

## Milt Barber

Milt Barber has lived on a small farm in Delanson, New York all his life. In fact, he lives in the same house in which he was born. For a good part of his life he was a dairyman, milking 25-30 cows, twice a day for over 30 years. The amazing fact that he missed only 2 milkings in those 30 years shows the kind of commitment Milt brings to his work. Dairy farming is hard, seven-days-a-week work. The cows are always there. The milkings at sunrise and sunset, the toil of producing hay, corn and silage and the myriad of farm chores like cleaning up after the herd and fixing equipment is a never ending battle. Milt did this all without the use of a hired hand, partly because dairy farming is not very rewarding financially, and partly because dairy farming is one of the few farm occupations remaining that allows an independent man and his family to till the soil and eke out an existence.

In recent years the cows have gone and the 130 acres of manure rich soil is used in production of row crops like sweet corn and tomatoes. Milt takes his work seriously, but grows pumpkins only for fun. In fact, in 1991, when he grew the third largest pumpkin in the world at 730.5 pounds and the 7th largest all time, he spent many weeks without so much as a glance to see how his plant was doing. That giant pumpkin measured 2 inches short of 14 feet, and was the largest circumference pumpkin grown in 1991.

About 5 years ago, Milt got started on a dare from an in-law, John James. John gave him some Atlantic Giant seeds and a $50 wager on the upcoming year's crop. John has never beat him since, despite the fact that he was the regional champ for many years before introducing Milt to the sport.

Milt Barber is the exception to the rule in the world of giant pumpkin growers. He does nothing special, except purchase good seed, and pays no particular attention to his plants. The sweet corn and the tomatoes come first, the pumpkins last. If there is too much work, the pumpkins are left to fend for themselves. No doubt the soil on which his pumpkins are grown is rich in organic matter, and the pest, disease and weed management practices he applies elsewhere on the farm also carry over to the pumpkins. As you can see, there really is more to his story than meets the eye. Milt is a grower who takes his skills, abilities and experiences for granted. Like most of us who toil daily at our work, we often fail to see the importance of what we do, and the skill with which we carry it out. Milt sees clearly what is important, namely good seed, good soil, sunshine and temperature. No doubt, Milt pays pretty good attention to all these factors.

Milt really came out of nowhere to enter the ranks of world class pumpkin growers, and based on his years of growing and soil management experience, he may be around for many more years.

When asked how old he was, he said,

> *"I'm a little to young for Medicare*
>
> *And a little too old for the women to care."*

If you would like to write to Milt, address your letters to: Milton Barber, RD #1, Delanson, New York 12053

*Top: Milt with friends and officials at a small village weighoff. This pumpkin lost almost 13 pounds in two weeks before being weighed in Collins, NY at the WPC Championship.*
*Below: Milt poses before cutting his Atlantic Giant from the vine.*

## Mark Woodward

Mark Woodward grew the first New England pumpkin over 700 pounds with a 718-pounder in 1992. This pumpkin dispelled the myth that New England weather could not produce world class pumpkins. Mark, with his wife Kathy, has been growing giant pumpkins since 1978. The 12 acre farm they live on and call home is kept up by summer haying, the pasturing of a few cows and a large family vegetable garden. Mark grows 4-5 Atlantic Giant Pumpkin plants each year. He believes in letting the seed do its thing, and is not overly obsessed with the passion to grow a giant every year.

*"If it comes, it comes."*

Mark does provide the best environment for growing by plowing down lots of compost made from manure mixed with leaves gathered around town in the fall. He only gets excited about pumpkin growing when he sees a potentially large one in the patch, and only then does he commit himself thoroughly to the task.

In 1987 he had a really good pumpkin growing. He estimated its weight at about 475 pounds in early September, which was very large back then. It had perfect shape and color, but unfortunately his cows noticed the same things. One jumped the garden fence and ate about 20 pounds before being noticed by the children. This pumpkin never made it to a weigh-off, but the seed from it produced a 507 pounder the next year.

Mark encourages other growers to be less serious about the sport and concentrate on basic gardening know-how. All you need is,

*"A garden with space, lots of sun, well prepared soil,*
*a water source and the commitment to stick with it*
*from May to October."*

If you would like to write to Mark or Kathy, address your inquiries to Mark Woodward, Brown Avenue., Leominster, Massachusetts 01453.

*Top: Mark slowly adjusts the position of one of his pumpkins to accommodate its accelerating growth.*
*Middle: End-of-season protection can add 2–3 weeks of growing time to the New England Fall, and help protect a prized pumpkin right up until weighoff day.*
*Right: Mark and Kathy Woodward behind the first over-700-pound pumpkin ever grown in New England. This pumpkin weighed 718 pounds and easily won the NEPGA weighoff at the Topsfield Fair in Topsfield, MA.*

## Alan Nesbitt

Alan Nesbitt is young for a world class pumpkin grower at only 22 years of age, but he has been in the top echelons of the sport since 1986 when he was only 16 years old. He is one of the few pumpkin growers today that have grown consistently large pumpkins and squash each and every season over a long period of time. This consistency leads me to believe that Alan will be around for many years to come and will be a future world record holder. He has the drive and the ability to do it. Alan grows both giant squash and giant pumpkins, and has done very well with both since 1986. His list of accomplishments in only 7 years is very impressive including:

1986 — 3rd largest pumpkin in the world and New York State record, 579.5 pounds

1989 — 3rd largest squash in the world, 589 pounds

1990 — 2nd largest squash in the world, 715.5 pounds

1991 — Largest squash in the world, 764 pounds.

He is one of only two men to have grown two 700-pound squash in separate years — the other being Len Stellpflug of Rush, New York.

In world championships, he has had 4 different years in which he has placed in the top 3 in the world for either squash or pumpkins. This is a feat worthy of a true Heavy Hitter.

Alan feels that 1986 was a pivotal year for competitive pumpkin growers. Since then, records have been destroyed almost every year, and with growers producing consistent 700–800 pound winners, the 1000 pound pumpkin cannot be very far in the future. Alan hopes that the first 1000-pound pumpkin does not come too soon. The quest has stirred up a lot of interest in the sport and more and more people are growing pumpkins and joining organizations affiliated with the sport. I think that the 1000 pound pumpkin will be grown in the next 5-10 years — and the interest in it will draw thousands of backyard growers into the sport.

If you would like to write to this young, energetic and successful grower, simply address your inquiry to : Alan Nesbitt, 5398 Turkey Hill Road, Conesus, New York 14435

## Don Fleming

Don Fleming of Morrisville, Vermont may very well be the most color- ful of all the Heavy Hitters. He burst onto the scene in 1986 and then won the World Championship in 1987 with a 604.5-pound pumpkin. He has made his presence felt to any pumpkin grower within earshot ever since.

His devotion to the sport is fanatical at times. Don is a true purist who expounds the sport as clean, wholesome fun for all. The motivation for him, as it is for most within the ranks of competitive pumpkin growing, is the 1000-pound quest. Prize money, fame, notoriety and other material compen- sation for growing giant pumpkins is meaningless to him without the quest, the fellowship of other growers and the constant obsession with the sport.

In 1986, David Letterman called Don and wanted him to come to New York City so his giant pumpkin could be thrown off a tall building (the ulti- mate pumpkin smashing). Letterman offered him $1000 plus all expenses paid, but Don turned him down for the sheer reason that this would have degraded all competitive pumpkin growers and brought a distorted picture of pumpkin growing to anyone watching the show. Don, instead, made giant Jack O'Lanterns from his prize winning pumpkins for his family and neighborhood kids. This paragraph really sums up Don's personality and attitudes toward the sport of pumpkin growing.

> *"The reason most people grow giant pumpkins is because they like to work in a garden for relaxation and for the enjoyment of growing things. That's the biggest part, and then to grow something really big. Pumpkins get the biggest! And then for the fun of it and some recognition, but never for profit."*

In 1986 and 1987 when Don was on top of the pumpkin growing world, he gave all of the seeds from these prize winning pumpkins to other grow- ers, mailing them at his own expense.

*Left Page:*

*Top: Alan Nesbitt at 16 with the New York State record and the 3rd largest pumpkin ever grown before 1986.*
*Middle: Alan in his pumpkin patch just prior to harvesting.*
*Bottom: Alan with his 733-pound world championship squash in 1991.*

*Right Page:*

*Top: Don Fleming transformed his world championship pumpkin in 1987 into the largest Jack O'Lantern ever carved at 604.5 pounds.*
*Below: Don with his winning entry at the Topsfield Fair.*
*Right: A rear shot of a large Jack O'Lantern.*

Personally, Don has meant a great deal to me. After reading an Associated Press newspaper story about the 1991 Topsfield Fair in Topsfield, Massachusetts, my interest was teased for more information on pumpkin growing. Unfortunately, the names and addresses of growers competing at the fair were incomplete in the story. In most cases I directed correspondence to only a name in a town, never expecting anything like what I received about 6 weeks later. I received a telephone call about 6 PM on a Friday night from a man living about 300 miles away. He introduced himself as Don Fleming, and immediately began feeding me information about giant pumpkin growing, the sport, the organizations and the key people to get to know. He even phoned some of them on my behalf so that I would receive whatever information was available on growing giant pumpkins and seed sources. A few weeks later I received a cordial letter, a packet of information and some seeds from Don. I considered this a totally unselfish act, and as I look back, it was a pivotal point in my life in which I chose to turn down the path of competitive pumpkin growing. At the time, I had no intentions of ever writing a book on pumpkins, but within a year, with the help of that Friday night phone call, this book became crystallized in my mind.

Everyone who enters this sport will be guided initially, in some way, by someone from within the ranks. Someone will show the newcomer how to join the organization, where to get seeds and how to get started. Each new grower will have a special person that will be his mentor, and he will remember this person for the rest of his life. For me it will always be Don Fleming — a champion pumpkin grower and a champion man.

If you wish to write to Don, address inquiries to :Don Fleming, RR2, Box 4800, Morrisville, Vermont 05661

*Above: World's heaviest Jack O'Lantern in 1987.*
*Right: Don and Elinor Fleming with a 530-pound pumpkin which won easily at the Topsfield Fair in 1986.*

Spons

## Hugh Wiberg

Hugh Wiberg has been a driving force within the World Pumpkin Confederation and the New England Pumpkin Growers Association for many, many years. He is well respected within the circle of competitive pumpkin growers as the ultimate gentleman, consummate organizer and fairest of judges. Hugh has been the site coordinator for the Topsfield Fair Weigh-off site, the Director of the New England Pumpkin Growers Association and a frequent contributor to the WPC and NEPGA member newsletters. Hugh has introduced many to the sport of pumpkin growing and is deserving of much praise for his significant contributions to the sport.

Hugh's largest pumpkin was a joint effort between himself and Tom Cone of Andover, Massachusetts in 1992. It weighed 582 pounds, and as I said earlier, The Heavy Hitters of the sport of pumpkin growing are not always those people who grow the largest pumpkins. Hugh's years of service in rallying New England growers has shown his zeal for the sport and his love for fellow pumpkin growers. Tom Cone also deserves much praise for his work within organized pumpkin growing and his growing of giant pumpkins. People behind the scenes, such as Tom, are the real reason why growers come to enjoy the comradery of the sport as much as the sport itself.

Hugh, Tom and others, were instrumental in creating the NEPGA and guided the organization through some tough years when many would have given up the sport entirely. Like most weigh-off site coordinators around the world, Hugh keeps a constant flow of information, both written and oral, moving amongst the growers. Small regional pumpkin growing organizations seem to be the wave of the future, because growers feel a closer bond with the membership, and also feel that they can give and receive more from these small groups. Most of these small pumpkin growing groups have been organized for purely humanitarian reasons. Most of them run fund raisers in conjunction with the annual weigh-off and spread the goodness of pumpkin growing to local people. These small organizations, networked into larger regional and world grower organizations like the WPC will create great opportunities for all growers as it relates to communication of information and verification of weights. I feel that Hugh will be at the forefront of these new developments as he has for the past 10 years.

Hugh has been growing giant pumpkins for over 30 years and up until 1971, his Big Max pumpkins were the talk of the neighborhood children. Most of these averaged between 150-175 pounds, but in 1971 an accidental cross with a Giant Hungarian Squash the previous season produced a fruit weighing about 280 pounds. This was very large for the time. The world record at this time was William Warnock's 1903 St. Louis World's Fair winner at 403 pounds. He dubbed his accidental cross "Squmpkin" (and he is thus given credit for coining the name which describes a half pumpkin half squash). For many years after, he freely distributed the seed through a Boston radio talk show devoted to the subject of backyard vegetable gardening. He also displayed these oddities at the Topsfield Fair, where he won numerous awards for heaviest cucurbit many times. His heaviest weighed about 375 pounds. His focus on the squmpkin and his generous

Above: Tom Cone, right, and Hugh Wiberg, Left, congratulate each other on their joint effort in growing the 2nd place winner at the 1992 Topsfield Fair. This pumpkin, their largest, weighed 582 pounds. Walter Carey, president of New Milford Farms, the 1992 sponsor of the Topsfield Pumpkin Weigh-off is center.

distribution of seed helped to create an awareness of large cucurbits in New England that otherwise would never have occurred

In the late seventies, the era of the Dill's Atlantic Giant was just beginning to collect momentum, and Hugh eagerly joined it. He has been exclusively growing the Atlantic Giant since 1980.

Hugh suggests that new growers be patient during the growing season. Too much fertilizer is far worse than too little. Slow and steady wins the race! Also, some kind of shade protection for the pumpkin fruit should be constructed soon after it reaches the size of a basketball. Giant pumpkins do not like direct sunlight and the intense heat of July and August. Growers in the south should pay particular attention to this advice.

Hugh is a published author, writing *Backyard Vegetable Gardening for the Beginner in* 1972 and is currently writing a book titled *Hand Feeding Wild Birds* which will be published in 1993 by Annedawn Publishing, Box 247-Bird, Norton, MA 02766.

If you care to write to Hugh concerning pumpkins or hand-feeding wild birds, address correspondence to: Hugh Wiberg, 445 Middlesex Avenue, Wilmington, Massachusetts 01886

*Right: Hugh Wiberg and Tom Cone pose for pictures to the right of New England Champions, Kathy and Mark Woodward with Gerry Griffin, the third place winner, to the far left.*

## Jerry McGowan

Jerry McGowan has been growing giant pumpkins for many years, and got his start, as many fathers do, growing a big pumpkin for his children. Jerry's daughter, as a little girl, asked him to grow her a big pumpkin. Even Jerry is amazed at where this seemingly insignificant request has lead him.

*Left: Jerry McGowan with his 704-pound entry at the WPC weighoff in Collins, NY.*

In 1991 Jerry grew the 13th largest pumpkin ever grown. His 704 pounder was the 5th largest in the world, and one of only thirteen pumpkins to ever top the 700 pound barrier.

A Vice President and Director in the stock exchange firm of Trubee, Collins and Company, Jerry proves that pumpkin growers do come from many walks of life. Jerry lives in Buffalo, NY, but tends his pumpkins on a small farm, one half mile north of Buffalo, New York in Ontario, Canada.

Jerry prides himself in advancing the sport by selectively breeding pumpkins with characteristics he particularly likes. For him, symmetry, color and good looks are as important as weight. He is personally sick of what many competitive pumpkin growers call the "blob look". The blob look, where the pumpkin weight is high but its shape is very low, resembles a pancake, and does nothing to conjure the real image of a round, carved Jack O'Lantern. I tend to agree with him. Jerry's sentiments reflect that of many growers who believe that winning-weights and prize money are secondary to the enjoyment one receives from growing a pumpkin that is beautiful to behold as well as being large.

*Right:"The Water Caper" was solved when two small holes were spotted in the stem of suspiciously heavy pumpkin. Surgical tubing was used by two pranksters to pump hundreds of pounds of water into the cavity of their pumpkin.*

Jerry was lucky enough to "snap" the picture above which shows to what extent some unscrupulous people will go to increase the weight of their pumpkin entry. This grower pumped hundreds of pounds of water into his pumpkin using surgical steel tubing inserted at the stem. Fortunately, this is an isolated instance of attempted fraud, and was discovered prior to any official weigh-in.

Jerry likes to share and swap seed with other growers in his attempt to combine the best characteristics of any large pumpkins grown. He offers these words of wisdom to new growers.

*"Plunge right in. Do not be timid. Go for it."*

He believes that only through growing pumpkins and recognizing your mistakes will you learn how to grow giant pumpkins.

For those of you who wish to correspond with Jerry, you may direct your inquiries to: Gerard McGowan, c/o Trubee, Collins and Company, Room 1350, One M & T Plaza, Buffalo, New York 14203

## Donald Black

Donald Black may very well be the most intense pumpkin grower of all time, yet to talk to him, you feel as if you are in the company of an old friend. Don is the "Keeper of the Seeds", and has spent the last 3 years writing and talking to anyone who has grown a pumpkin over 400 pounds, and then cataloging and archiving any seed that is received. His noble mission is to protect the seed stock from any catastrophe and catalog seed lineage. To date, Don has about 200 different seed stocks archived.

His knowledge of who grew what, when and where is amazing. Any conversation with him will be a whirl of numbers as he describes a pumpkin, its "parents" and its "offspring" with a blast of 3-digit numbers. He knows the lineage and seed offspring history of just about every major pumpkin grown in the world in the last 3-4 years, and has many of them in his archives.

I asked Don to give me his opinion of the 5 best seed stocks to seek out for high probability giant pumpkins. He explained that there were many good candidates, but after a few minutes of verbal shuffling, he had outlined the five for me. He also warned that these seed stocks may already be depleted, or in such short supply that owners of them may be reluctant to part with any of them.

Nevertheless, the question stirred up his adrenaline, and out came the following "Best Five" list:

#1 — Howard Dill's 1988, 575-pounder. Don considers this seed stock to be the most valuable. Among its offspring is the present world record, grown by Joel Holland in 1992, at 827 pounds.

#2 — Howard Dill's 1988, 616-pounder. Its offspring includes Gordon Thomson's 755-pound world record pumpkin of 1989 which smashed the existing world record by 84 pounds, broke the 700-pound barrier for the first time and beat everyone in North America by a whopping 114 pounds. Don considers the 755 as being one of the most beautiful and impressive pumpkins ever grown. Except for a small depression in the top of the pumpkin, it exhibited all of the best characteristics of great, giant pumpkins. It had good height, good breadth, beautiful color and a uniformity of shape unmatched by any previous world record pumpkin.

#3 —Mike MacDonald's 1991, 717.5-pounder. The seed from this pumpkin produced many 700-plus-pound pumpkins in 1992, and in general, all exhibited the characteristics most sought by today's competitive pumpkin growers — good shape, good color and high weight.

#4 — Gordon Thomson's 1989, 467-pounder.

#5 — Ed Gancarz's, 530-pounder. The seed from this pumpkin produced the 816.5-pound, 1990 world record pumpkin and many other 700-pound-plus pumpkins since.

Don adds that there are many other good seed sources and warns against putting too much faith in any one grower's seed. Grow seed from several sources each year to reduce the chance of disappointing results. He also heartily advises purchasing seed directly from Howard Dill. He con-

*Top: Donald Black in his pumpkin patch in Winthrop, NY. Below: Gordon Thomson's 1989, 755-pound pumpkin which Don describes as one of the most beautiful world championship pumpkin ever grown.*

*Top: Don Black with Gerry Griffin of Amston, CT.*
*Below: Don readies his patch for some late season protection.*

siders Howard to be the very best breeder of Atlantic Giant pumpkins in the world and any of his seed stocks have high probability of producing truly giant pumpkins with good color and shape. He suggests purchasing some of Dill's seed then mix in a couple of other growers like Joel Holland (who is the current world record holder and has had good results the last few years) and Ray Waterman. P & P Seed Co. was mentioned as having two very good seed stocks. Ray's 674.5-pound and 742-pound pumpkin seed stocks were recommended as having real potential. The 674.5 was responsible for Mike MacDonald's 717.5 mentioned as Don's #3 choice for seed stock. It was also responsible for Ray Waterman and Ayo Ogungbuyi's 1991, 780.5-pounder, which is the third largest pumpkin ever grown.

Don started growing pumpkins in 1988 when he saw an article about giant pumpkins on the back page of his local newspaper. From this article he received Don Fleming's address, and from Don he received directions on how to get in touch with Howard Dill. He bought seed from Howard in January of 1988 and brought a 143-pounder to the WPC weigh-off site in Collins, New York that Fall. He placed third from the bottom and as he said it,

*"That kind of ticked me off."*

The very next day he called Howard and pleaded for some better seed for the 1989 season. Howard sent him seed from the now famous 616. In 1989, Don grew his largest pumpkin, a 625-pounder which ranks him in the top 30 pumpkins all time. Don has also had good results with giant squash, growing a 571 pounder in 1992, which was 5th in the world.

Don figures that the sport's elite growers have all grown 700-pound pumpkins and believes that by the end of 1993 this elite class will only include growers who have grown 800-pound pumpkins. He predicts that a 1000-pound pumpkin will be grown before the year 2000, but also predicts that a giant squash will break the 1000-pound barrier first.

Don spends an average of 50 hours per week during the growing season tending his plants. He works very hard and plays very hard, but will always remain a great guy to be around.

If you wish to correspond with Don, address inquiries to: Donald Black, Box 192, Rt. 1, Winthrop, New York 13697

Include your phone number, because, in true form, Don would rather talk to you in person.

## Joel Holland

Joel Holland has been growing giant pumpkins for only 6 years but during that time he has grown two, 600-pound pumpkins, one 700-pounder and one 800-pounder. His improvement has been phenomenal, from 244 pounds in 1987 to 827 pounds and a world record in 1992.

Joel believes that,

> "*Careful attention to details and sound cultural practices ultimately leads to success. Seek counsel from experienced growers who have been successful, especially growers in your area. Certain principles may be fairly universal, but there are many timing issues and other matters which can be highly regional specific.*"

Joel serves to remind me that many thousands of people will be reading this book, and many of them will not be growing pumpkins under the same conditions as New England. His point of observing regional timing issues is very, very important. Frost dates and average daytime high and low temperatures are variables which will have to be approached on a personal level. Each grower will have to adjust planting, pollination and protection schedules as they relate to his region. Growing in New England is very different than growing in the Pacific Northwest, the Mid-Atlantic Seaboard, the Deep South and so on. Joel goes on to say,

*Above: Joel with the world record pumpkin weighed at the WPC Nut Tree weigh-off in Vacaville, CA in 1992. This giant weighed-in at an amazing 827 pounds.*
*Below: Joel poses with his winning entry at the Half Moon Bay Pumpkin Festival which set a new site record at 722 pounds in '92.*

> "*When I started, the popular wisdom coming from the East Coast said to set out plants between May 15th and June 1st and pollinate between July 15th and August 1st. When I followed that schedule in the maritime Northwest, I found my pumpkins did not reach their full potential. We have very limited daytime heating with average highs in July of 75 degrees and lows in the 50's, usually the low 50's. Our pumpkins grow at a slower rate than some areas, but will grow over a longer season. My world record, 827 pound pumpkin was harvested 96 days after pollination. From day 89 through day 96 it was growing at an average of five pounds per day. I've pushed my target planting date back to the first week in May, and the pollination date back to late June / early July. This probably would not work in some warmer areas, as a grower might wind up with a mature specimen around September 1st and have to contend with holding the pumpkin in condition for a month.*"

Joel also believes strongly in a,

> "*Thoughtful, long term program of building soil fertility.*"

Attention to soil structure, pH and nutrient levels are very important, along with monitoring and maintaining adequate levels of phosphorous. Also, avoid walking on soil around your plants. Soil compacting can lead to restrictive root growth. Joel uses wide boards.

Joel advises that growers not act hastily in their final fruit selection process. He likes to hand-pollinate 4-6 female blossoms that have 4–6 stigmas (referred to as blossom segments or lobes in this book). His world record, 827-pound pumpkin originated from a 5-stigma-blossom. Joel usually eliminates 2–3 fruits during the first two weeks of observation, and lets the remaining fruit grow for another 2-3 weeks.

*"I often let the 2–3 finalists grow to 50–60 pounds before making the final selection."*

During this 2-3 weeks, he looks for the ideal pumpkin which will be high and rounded and possess smooth, glossy skin. He measures each finalist, each day and makes comparisons. At this stage he looks for the fruit that attains the greatest increase in size on a per day basis.

*"A one-quarter to one-half-inch difference in circumference growth per day, at this stage, can translate into the difference between a good specimen and a world class specimen by the end of the season. Neither my 827-pound or 722-pound pumpkins were the largest on their respective plants when selected, but each was growing at the highest rate."*

Besides size and color, Joel advises observing,

*"Size and health of the vine, diameter and length of the stem, position of the pumpkin and distance from the main root."*

*Above: Joel with a 616-pound 1st-Place Winner at the Nut Tree Weighoff in 1991.*
*Below: The "Harvest Crew" takes some time for this picture of Joel's 1992 pumpkin and squash specimens. (front right–827-pound pumpkin, front left–722-pound pumpkin, back right–592-pound pumpkin and back left–608-pound squash.*

Joel prunes his plants starting at a young age to limit sprawl.

*"You need to encourage a balance between vine growth and fruit production."*

You must manage stem stress by training downstream vines away from the pumpkin to create space for the pumpkin to grow, and sever anchor roots, in both directions on the vine around the fruit, to reduce stem stress.

At 44, Joel has been a firefighter in the Puyallup, Washington municipal fire department for 22 years and has been nurturing his nephew, Matt Holland's interest in giant pumpkins since 1989. Matt beat Joel in 1989 with a 433-pounder. Matt has also grown a 578, 594 and 592-pound pumpkins in successive years, and is showing the same steady improvement as his uncle.

If you would like to write to Joel or Matt, you may address inquiries to: Joel Holland, 9422 144th Street East, Puyallup, Washington 98373-6686

*Above: Joel relaxes with his daughter, Shawn and his grandson, Jacob. Matt Holland's 1992, 592-pounder is the subject of pride.*
*Left Top: Joel with the current world record pumpkin just prior to harvesting.*
*Left Bottom: Joel and Matt Holland in 1990 with Joel's 605-pound pumpkin and Matt's 578-pounder.*

## Mike MacDonald

Mike MacDonald started growing giant pumpkins in 1989 after seeing many articles about Howard Dill and his pumpkins. He ordered some Dill's Atlantic Giant seeds from a seed catalog and plunged headlong into the endeavor. Although he lives on a dairy/market-garden farm, and grows 2 acres of squash and pumpkins, he had never had any experience growing giant pumpkins. In his first year, he grew a 153 pounder which was quite large for his region, but Gordon Thomson's 755 pound pumpkin was the world champion and new world record holder. By chance, Mike got to meet Gordon, discussed pumpkin growing and walked away with renewed interest and enthusiasm for the sport. As he said,

*"I had to think of what my limitations were. It was not climate (Gordon Thomson lives only 80 miles away from me), not space (300 acres of land to plant), not lack of cow manure (always an abundance on a dairy farm), not water (irrigation pond that gravity feeds right to the pumpkin patch) and not good seed (Howard Dill is very generous with his good seed). Looking back now, I realize that my only limitations were experience and pumpkin plant know-how. The basic thing that one has to do is to provide optimum conditions for growth at all times to the best of your ability."*

Below: Mike MacDonald in 1991 with his famous 717.5-pounder.

In 1990, he ordered seed directly from Howard Dill, improved some of his growing techniques and grew a 480 pounder which was weighed at the WPC weigh-off site in Collins, NY. It finished tied for 22nd place. On seeing the pumpkins of Robert and Edward Gancarz (765 and 816.5 pounds), he figured that those weights would be forever out of his reach.

In 1991, he gave his plants more room, and with the luck of good Summertime weather, grew a 717.5-pound pumpkin. This pumpkin placed 4th in the WPC weigh-off, catapulted him into the WPC Top 30 All Time Pumpkins group and as he says,

*"All of a sudden, I was amongst the big boys."*

This initiation into the ranks of the upper echelon of competitive pumpkin growers gave him many opportunities to speak directly with the top growers and exchange ideas and philosophies on how to grow a world record pumpkin. He enjoys this very much.

Incidentally, the seeds from Mike's 717.5-pounder have grown many 700+ pound pumpkins including three top-5 finishers at the 1992 New England Championship at the Topsfield Fair weigh-off site in Topsfield, Massachusetts. Don Black, a well respected authority on the Dill's Atlantic Giant seed stock, rates the seed from the 717.5-pounder as one of the top 5 seed stocks existing today.

Mike feels that the first ten days after germination is the most critical time for the plant. He germinates seed in 4" peat pots, no earlier than May 1st, inside a cold frame heated by a space heater. The heater keeps the temperature at a constant 65–70 degrees at all times. Since pumpkin seedlings are very sensitive to restricted root growth, he transplants the seedlings to the pumpkin patch within 5–6 days of germination.

He spaces plants 60' x 20', lets all the main and secondary vines go, and trims off all of the tertiary vines. He buries all the vines with soil and tries to train them in an orderly way. He waters sparingly using overhead sprinklers. He spreads about 200 bushels of cow manure for each plant in the preceding Fall, another 100 bushels in Spring, plus 30 pounds of 10-10-10 fertilizer. During the summer he fertilizes with water soluble formulations delivered through his sprinkler system. He tests for soil salinity throughout the summer. If the dissolved concentration of salts is high, he waters copiously without the use of any water soluble fertilizer. If salt concentrations are low, he uses higher concentrations of fertilizer through this irrigation system.

Mike feels relieved that he lives far enough north so that he is not plagued by the dreaded Squash Vine Borer. He focuses his insect and disease controls on Cucumber and Flea Beetles and Powdery Mildew. He uses Rotenone and Benomyl to control these pests.

Mike was born in Sherbrooke on December 9, 1963, grew up on the farm his Grandfather purchased in 1933 — and all his family, from both sides, have been in the area for nearly 150 years.

If you would like to write to Mike, address your inquiries to: Mike MacDonald 696 MacDonald Road, Sherbrooke, Quebec, Canada J1H 5G9.

## Leonard Stellpflug

Len Stellpflug has been competing in the WPC weigh-offs since 1986 and has grown a 645 pound pumpkin. He has earned his stature as a heavy hitter  not only by growing world class pumpkins, and world record squash but also by his contributions to the sport from the research and development side. Len is a frequent contributor to the WPC's newsletter which is read by everyone-who-is-anyone in the world of competitive pumpkin growing.

Len is credited with developing a measurement system for estimating the weight of giant pumpkins and squash which the WPC has copyrighted. This system is used extensively by all competitive growers who track daily weight gains. Len was generous enough to allow his research to become public knowledge through his frequent writings. He continues ongoing research of his theories by factoring-in new data each year received from pumpkin growers all over the world. With a BS and MS in Engineering, Len appears well qualified to manage this research.

*Above: Len Stellpflug with an 807-pound squash in 1990 which won the WPC Giant Squash Championship and was the largest squash ever grown.*
*Right: Len with a pumpkin just prior to harvest in 1991. This pumpkin was officially weighed at Collins, NY at 645 pounds.*

Len is, without doubt, the best giant squash grower in the world. For the past four years he has been listed in the *Guinness Book of World Records.* He has set three world records in the squash category including a 653.5-pounder in 1988, a 743 pounder in 1989 and a 821 pounder in 1990.

Len's goal is to grow a 1000 pound pumpkin or squash.

## Gordon Thomson

There have been very few people who have made an impact on pumpkin growing like Gordon Thomson. After retiring in 1985, Gordon's thoughts were on relaxing, and perhaps growing a small kitchen garden behind the house. A seed catalog perked his interest in the Dill's Atlantic Giant, and since he had already heard of Howard Dill and giant pumpkins, he decided to grow one. Using, as he says, "Seed-house seed," he grew a 192-pound pumpkin in 1986. This caused quite a stir in Hemmingford, Quebec, Canada despite the fact that Robert Gancarz grew a world record 671-pounder in 1986. This shows how little people actually knew about the sport and the achievements within it. Gordon Thomson would have a hand in transforming this little-known sport, and along the way, helping millions of people to understand the achievements which pumpkin growers were having. In 1987, Gordon grew another pumpkin with much the same results as that of his previous year. He decided to call Howard Dill and get seed directly from him instead of from a catalog. In 1988, using Howard's seed, he grew a 450-pounder which he brought to Collins, New York for the WPC weigh-off. That same year, Howard Dill grew a 616-pound pumpkin which has since received much recognition for the seedling offspring it has produced. Gordon was smart enough, and lucky enough, to recognize the potential of the 616, and in 1989, he planted seed from it. In the Fall, Gordon made the long trip to Collins, New York, but this time he knew he had a potential winner in tow. Don Fleming had made a trip to Hemmingford, measured the pumpkin and began immediately spreading the word of a potential new world record coming from Gordon's backyard. As prophesied, Gordon's pumpkin did win the WPC weigh-off in Collins in 1989, but the extent of that victory sent ripples through the pumpkin grow-ing world. Gordon had not only broken the 700-pound barrier, he had shat-tered it with a mammoth 755-pound pumpkin. It destroyed the previous world record by 84 pounds. This pumpkin was also not your average, oblong shaped mass. The 755 was perhaps the most beautiful world record giant pumpkin specimen ever grown. It had good height, breadth and color.

Gordon was immediately besieged by media types, businessmen and growers in search of a story, a promotional angle for their business or seed. He decided to lend his pumpkin to a Baltimore, Maryland, businessman who would display it to thousands of onlookers over a two week period. When Gordon went to retrieve his pumpkin, he knew that it had begun to rot. Baltimore is just too hot for holding pumpkins in October. The pump-kin had shrunk noticeably, and its high, rounded profile now seemed to sag under the weight of its outer shell. When he opened the 755 to retrieve its seed, he found a real mess. Most of the seed had already begun to germi-nate, and those that had not, were stewing in a rotten liquor at the base of the pumpkin's giant cavity. He carefully removed them, but found only 20–30 suitable for keeping.

In 1990, none of these seeds succeeded in germinating. He met the Baltimore businessman again at the WPC weigh-off in Collins in the Fall, and learned that he had salvaged seven seeds from the 755, and would glad-ly return them to Gordon. In 1991, he succeeded in germinating one of the

*Gordon Thomson's World Record Pumpkin shocked the world of competitive pumpkin growing. This was the first pumpkin to break the 700-pound barrier at 755 pounds.*
*Below: Don Fleming examines the famous "755" prior to harvest in October 1989.*

seven, and about mid-season had a great looking plant growing with a very big pumpkin set on it. Gordon remarked at the time,

*"Here we go again"*,

but it was not to be. You see, this pumpkin was not only green, it was as Gordon calls it,

*"Green as grass."*

It soon suffered from blossom end rot, ending all hope for the offspring of one of the most publicized pumpkins of all time.

The ripples that the 755 set in motion in the world of pumpkin growing have not subsided to this very day. For the first time, growers actually believed that a 1000-pound pumpkin could be possible, and this belief has motivated pumpkin growers and brought more and more people into the sport.

Gordon has taken all of this pretty much in stride, and continues to grow giant pumpkins with the same enthusiasm he had when he first started. As he says,

*"You need good seed, good soil, good weather and good luck."*

Let's all hope that we are not only lucky enough to grow a big one, but also lucky enough to see its offspring.

*Above: Gordon accepts the winning plaque from WPC President Ray Waterman in 1989 at the Collins, NY, World Pumpkin Weigh-Off.*
*Right: Gordon and his wife pose behind the first pumpkin to break the 700-pound barrier.*

## Al Eaton

Al Eaton is a thoroughly committed grower of giant pumpkins. "Bitten by the bug" in 1988, his yearly pumpkin weights have grown from 259 pounds to 661 pounds in 1992, and his enthusiasm for the sport has likewise increased.

Al is fascinated with numbers and the proper communication of pumpkin weights and ranks. He even started a statistical clearing house for weigh-off sites which tabulates pumpkin weights regardless of organizational affiliation. A site is qualified to submit data if the average of its top 10 pumpkins exceeds 400 pounds. The statistics collected from each site will be compiled and returned to each organization for inclusion in their local newsletter. In this way, the myriad of organizations and festival weigh-off sites can be accounted for, and a complete list of weights and ranks can be generated each year. All site coordinators are encouraged to write to Al for more details on the subject and anyone interested in writing to a very serious and committed grower of giant pumpkins should address his inquiries to Al Eaton, Box 1217, Richmond, Ontario, Canada K0A 2Z0.

*Below: Al Eaton grapples with his 681-pound pumpkin in 1992.*

## Norm Gallagher

Perhaps no one more epitomizes the virtues of a competitive pumpkin grower than Norm Gallagher. This 80-year-old giant in the world of giant pumpkin growing has been a source of inspiration for many in the sport. Alan Nesbitt, a Heavy Hitter himself, calls Norm "pure legend". With his lovely, energetic wife, Ruth, the Gallagher's have won many a heart at the Manson, Washington pumpkin weigh-offs.

Norm was the first man to break the 600-pound barrier with a 612-pound pumpkin in 1984. This pumpkin literally destroyed Howard Dill's 4-year-old world record of 493.5 pounds, and immediately earned Norm a place in the record books and in the hearts of all pumpkin growers. The "612" earned Norm and Ruth a $10,000 prize from the WPC and a trip to Hawaii.

The "612" was a historic feat. In one stroke a new world record was established and both the 500 and 600-pound barriers were broken. Perhaps no other pumpkin grower will duplicate this feat. It would be akin to someone growing a 1000-pound pumpkin in 1993 with no one coming closer than 700+ pounds.

Norm has semi-retired from the sport finding much enjoyment traveling to weigh-offs and always being there, with Ruth, to offer praise and encouragement to other growers.

If you would like to write to Norm or Ruth, address your inquiries to: Norman Gallagher, 706 East Wapato, Chelan, WA 98816.

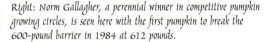

*Right: Norm Gallagher, a perennial winner in competitive pumpkin growing circles, is seen here with the first pumpkin to break the 600-pound barrier in 1984 at 612 pounds.*

## Edward and Robert Gancarz

The Gancarz Boys are legends in the world of competitive pumpkin growing. Both have set world records, won world championships and consistently performed well over many years. What they add to the world of competitive pumpkin growing is incalculable, because their mere presence brings out the very best in all growers.

Robert Gancarz set a world record in 1986 with a 671-pound pumpkin, and it remained the largest pumpkin ever grown until Gordon Thomson grew his historic "755" in 1989. Four years is a long time to hold a world record in pumpkin growing based on current conditions. It shows just how important his accomplishment was. Norm Gallagher's 612-pound pumpkin of 1984 is considered a landmark achievement, yet Robert's 671-pounder paved the way for the assault on the 700-pound barrier. Robert has also grown other notable pumpkins, and his year to year performance is the envy of all competitive pumpkin growers. All and all, Robert has 3 pumpkins in the WPC Top 30 All-Time category. In 1989 he grew a 619.5-pounder, in 1986, his world record 617-pounder, and in 1990, he grew the fourth largest pumpkin ever grown with a 765.5-pound specimen.

Likewise, Edward Gancarz has been at the top of competitive pumpkin growing for a long time. He was the first to break the 800-pound barrier with a 816.5-pound world record pumpkin in 1990, and he remains as one of only two men to grow an 800-pound pumpkin — the other being Joel Holland who holds the current world record at 827 pounds. Edward's 816.5 shattered a world record many thought was unsurpassable. Gordon Thomson's 755 was thought to be a rare event not likely to be repeated. Edward also holds the distinction of 3, Top 30 WPC All-Time pumpkins with a 641-pounder in 1989, a 618.5-pounder in 1986 and the historic "816.5".

Both Robert and Edward deserve much praise for their accomplishments, consistency and fierce competitiveness.

*Above: Robert Gancarz holds his world record, 671-pound pumpkin at the WPC Championship in Collins, NY in 1986.*
*Below: Edward Gancarz, left, inspects one of Alan Nesbitt's squash which took 2nd place worldwide in 1990 at 715.5 pounds.*
*Left: Ed Gancarz poses proudly next to his 1990, 816.5-pound world record pumpkin which was the first pumpkin to break the 800-pound barrier and the 2nd largest pumpkin ever grown to date.*
*Right: Ray Waterman proudly poses with one of his prized specimens. Photo courtesy of the WPC.*

Above: Dill's Atlantic Pumpkin Seeds compared to a dime.
Right Page
        Top: A package of Dill's Atlantic Giant Pumpkin Seeds.
        Bottom: Dill's Seed Catalog is available by writing to
        Howard Dill, 400 College Road, Windsor, Nova
        Scotia, Canada BON 2TO.

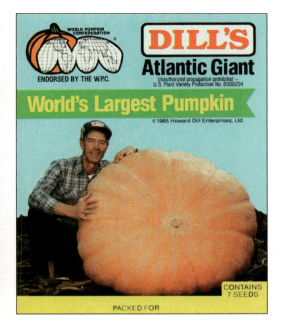

# Chapter 4 *Securing the Right Seed*

If you ask any good, competitive pumpkin grower the question, "What is the most important step I can take to increase my chances of growing a truly giant pumpkin?", you will almost always hear the answer, "Grow the right seed", and as an afterthought, "Get lucky!"

To put this last paragraph in perspective, you could spend your entire life improving your garden soil and improving the ways in which you grow pumpkins, but if you choose to grow Jack O'Lantern, Connecticut Field or other Halloween pumpkin varieties, you will never reach sizes even remotely resembling the Dill's Atlantic Giant. The inherent characteristics and genetic purity of a variety is inbred through many years of controlled growing and trials. Named varieties rarely display characteristics that are not normal to them. Connecticut Field pumpkins may reach weights of 50

**HALLOWEEN PUMPKIN GROWING TIPS**

1. Plant one packet of seed plants per 6 hills, four pounds of seed per acre.
2. The hills should be 8 to 10 feet apart thus allowing the vines plenty of room to grow.
3. Garden variety plants can be started indoors or directly seeded in late May or early June after the soil has warmed.
4. Dust plants regularly to protect against the cucumber beetle.
5. Pumpkins will take a light frost but don't leave them in the field too long as a freeze will affect keeping quality.

*These tips do not apply to the Atlantic Giant.*

PLEASE SEND
ORDER TO

**HOWARD DILL**
400 COLLEGE ROAD
WINDSOR, N.S.
CANADA  B0N 2T0
PHONE: 1-902-798-2728

MY CORRECT NAME AND ADDRESS:

NAME
ADDRESS
TOWN
POSTAL CODE
PROV.
PHONE

CATALOG NUMBER | HOW MANY | DESCRIPTION | PRICE

TOTAL ORDER
HANDLING   $1.00
GST 7%
**TOTAL**

PLEASE SEND A CHEQUE OR MONEY ORDER WITH YOUR ORDER. SORRY NO C.O.D.'S
CANADIAN RESIDENTS ADD 7% GST
PLEASE ALLOW 4-5 WEEKS FOR DELIVERY

## WELCOME TO THE WORLD OF PUMPKIN GROWING!

As a result of the many requests from gardeners over the past several years for a seed catalog, we are pleased to introduce our premier edition of the Dill Seed Catalog. Featured in the catalog are a variety of pumpkins which range in size from the world's smallest - "Jack-Be-Little" to the world's largest - "Atlantic Giant".

During the past decade pumpkin growing has developed a world-wide following and we trust that the varieties of pumpkins represented here will meet that world-wide demand.

If there are other varieties that interest you or if you have any suggestions that would help us to improve our service to you then please send us a letter. We're always interested in hearing from pumpkin growers!

Happy pumpkin growing,

*Howard Dill*

Howard Dill

PRODUCED BY EXCEL PUBLISHING, P.O. BOX 5240, HALIFAX, N.S. B3L 4S7. © DAVID TOWLER

# DILL'S

## SEED CATALOG

*Featuring seeds of the world's largest variety of pumpkin*

**ATLANTIC GIANT**

ENDORSED BY THE W.P.C.

pounds or more (their average is 25-40 pounds), but they will never reach 100, 200, 500 or 800 pounds. You have to grow seed that has the characteristics to grow that big.

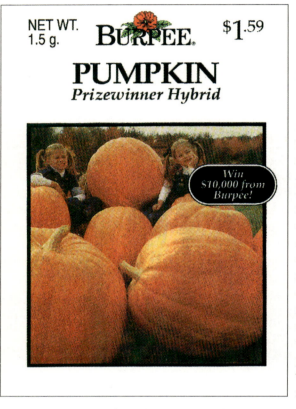

The Dill's Atlantic Giant and Burpee's Prizewinner are the only varieties grown by today's competitive pumpkin growers, and all the world records for the last 14 years have been attributed to the Atlantic Giant. Burpee's Prizewinner is normally planted by competitive growers only as a secondary crop. It has some very notable characteristics of beauty, which include good shape and color, but has yet to win a world championship or break any world pumpkin records.

*Left: A seed package of Burpee's Prizewinner promotes a $10,000 prize for a world championship pumpkin grown with its variety.*

There are a number of sources in which to purchase seed for the Dill's Atlantic Giant. Predominant among these sources is, of course, the developer and patent holder, Howard Dill and the "Dill-approved", P & P Seed Company. Dill grows seed at his Nova Scotia, Canada, home for retail sale. The rest of the commercially available seed is sold by various seed companies throughout the world. A list of seed suppliers appears in the appendix of this book. All seed companies selling Atlantic Giant seed receive permission from Dill. To date, about 20 acres of reproduction seed is grown in California and Colorado under the auspices of Dill. This seed serves more than 2 million gardeners who grow either competitively or as a hobby.

It is important to understand that the Dill's Atlantic Giant is a variety protected by the U.S Plant Variety Protection Act. The initials "PVP" appear on all seed packets that have been granted a PVP Certificate. In the case of the Dill's Atlantic Giant, Howard Dill, who developed the variety over 30 painstaking years, is the holder of the certificate, and no one else may sell seeds grown from an Atlantic Giant without his written permission. Trading seed, on a limited basis, is not generally objected to by a PVP certificate holder, but unlawful propagation and sale is.

As stated earlier, named varieties rarely display characteristics outside their normal ranges of expectancy, yet new world records seem to be broken every year or two using Atlantic Giant seeds. The reasons for this is the selective replanting of seed from the biggest pumpkins or those in which history has shown a high probability of good offspring. Whereas seed producing farms isolate varieties so as to not introduce new characteristics, competitive pumpkin growers strive to selectively cross larger pumpkins with still larger ones. They are all Atlantic Giants, but in some ways, the genes for each are slightly different or the predominance of one gene over another has been modified or changed. The challenge of growing larger pumpkins will always be with us, and the improvement of seed characteristics will be the only way we will meet this challenge.

Once a pumpkin grower grows a giant, world record, or near record pumpkin, other growers will flock to him for seed, however it should be noted that championship pumpkins have not shown a good history of producing seed that grew more championship pumpkins in subsequent years. In fact, no world championship pumpkin has ever produced offspring that exceeded or came close to its own weight. Instead, all of the world championships and world records have come from seed of lesser weight pumpkins. An understanding of what seed stocks will produce the highest probability of success is integral in the process of determining what seeds you should grow. What you choose to grow should be based on what is available from authorized propagators and your knowledge of seed stock track records.

Seed stocks that have fairly reliable results in producing large pumpkins come to be remembered by the size of the pumpkin that produced them. The jargon of pumpkin growers, therefore, revolves around numbers. They will talk about growing the "717", "742", "575" and so on. These numbers are used to differentiate the source of the seed. If you grow a world record pumpkin, like Joel Holland did in 1992, people will flock to you for your seeds. In the case of Joel, his seed will be remembered as the "827" because that was the weight of the pumpkin that produced them. Others will dig still deeper into the history of the 827, and will instead, seek seed from one of the parent pumpkins that produced it. Joel keeps good records of pollination, as do most successful growers. His 827 came from the cross-pollination of the 575 and the 742. The Dill's 575 was the mother (the female portion of the equation), and the Waterman 742 was the father. Each of these seed stocks escalated in popularity as a result of Joel's achievement and each will see increased, widespread use until their stocks are exhausted or other stocks are created which promise the potential for even greater weights.

My advice to new growers of giant pumpkins is to begin by purchasing seed from Howard Dill or other seed companies listed in the appendix of this book. After a season or two of growing, and a trip or two to a regional weigh-off, you will begin to see very clearly that growers are growing seed from seed stocks which have proved their ability to produce good offspring.

Most growers like you and me have very small garden plots that can only accommodate one or two hills. This means that you have to make some tough decisions over what to plant of all the seed that is available to you. A truly competitive grower will seek attributes that promise larger pumpkins. Besides weight, characteristics like increased height, length, wall thickness and improved color are characteristics which are sought by all growers of the Dill's Atlantic Giant.

*Below: Stokes Seed Company is also an authorized seller of the Dill's Atlantic Giant.*

## How do you secure the right seed?

Start by turning to the appendix of this book. Write to the seed companies listed. Ask for any literature they have on giant pumpkin growing, and of course, ask for their seed catalog. Purchase seed from an authorized seller of the Dill's Atlantic Giant, grow a pumpkin and join a pumpkin growing organization. Write for information on their annual weigh-off, then attend it with or without a pumpkin. A day with a group of serious pumpkin growers will change your life. You will make friendships that will last the rest of your life, and you will begin a learning process that will never end. From these friends and fellow competitors, you will receive all the knowledge you will ever need about How to Secure the Right Seed!

Remember that the more you know, the luckier you will get!

# Chapter 5 Choosing the Growing Area

Where you grow your giant pumpkin is an important deci-sion because giant pumpkins require a great deal from the soil and sun and a large area in which to do it. In addition, protection of these large plants can dramatically enhance their health and the size of the pumpkins they bear.

The single most important ingredient determining the suitability of a growing area is its exposure to the sun. Since many pumpkin growers are backyard gardeners, and American backyards have been shrinking for decades, the amount of good space in yards has been declining. Also the popularity of treed, residential house lots has also reduced the availability of good, full sun growing areas. A few mature trees on a small house lot can cut the amount of sunlight that reaches a pumpkin patch, either by screen-ing the early morning sun or the late afternoon and evening sunshine.

A good rule of thumb is to have complete exposure to the sun by 8 AM or before, and lasting until 6 PM or after. Anything less than this will reduce the energy requirements needed to grow a world-class, giant pumpkin. Solving the problem of underexposure to sun is not easy. Many of us are not ready to part with an old tree we have become accustomed to, and planting somewhere besides are own backyards may take the fun out of growing entirely, but many serious pumpkin growers grow their plants in areas not contained in their backyards. They have recognized the serious need for full sun, and have chosen to forego the convenience and satisfaction of growing close to their house. For them, this act punctuates their commitment to growing giant pumpkins. Some of them rent, or get permission to use old fields once planted to corn or alfalfa or some commercial crop. Most are old farms used for dairy cows where huge amounts of manure have been spread on the fields for generations. These fields rarely have problems with expo-sure to sun, however convenience to home and sources of water may make these locations difficult to work with. Also, vandalism can never be entirely ruled out. Only your desire to grow a truly giant pumpkin will determine the lengths to which you go in pursuit of the ideal growing area. If you do not have full sun in your backyard, and you wish to grow world-class giant pumpkins, you must look elsewhere to grow your plants.

Ask around. Friends and relatives are always interested in gardening, and the challenge of growing a giant pumpkin may intrigue them as well. Not only will you get a good piece of earth, but also a helping hand in the chores of preparing the soil and maintaining the patch through the growing season. And, just as important, you will be exposing another person to the sport of giant pumpkin growing.

Another important characteristic of a good growing area is its natural defenses against wind and frost. Natural screens like hedgerows or thickets will dramatically decrease the amount of wind on your plot. Protecting pumpkin plants from high wind is very important because the plants contain large leaves and many hundreds of them. These leaves catch the wind like sails on a sailboat. Wind can tear vines from the ground, break them, or at the very least, raise considerable havoc on the plant. Anything which reduces the elements of wind or any rapid air flow through the patch will benefit the plants and the pumpkins they bear. Many competitive growers erect windbreaks regardless of the natural conditions that exist. We will cover this practice in detail later in this book.

The elevation of your garden is also an important consideration. I am speaking about its relative elevation in your yard as opposed to your areas relative elevation compared to sea level. Low areas of your yard should be avoided if at all possible. In the micro climate of your yard, these low areas will historically be the coldest. They will receive the last frost in Spring and the first frost of Fall. It is easy to visualize why this is so. Picture your yard as a bowl. If you pour water into a bowl it fills it from the bottom first. When you think of air movement, gravity is not as important as temperature of the air. Remember that warm air rises and cold air sinks. When your yard encounters a cold, windless night, the air does not move haphazardly. It first floods the low areas, much like water poured into a bowl. Cold air moves to the lowest areas, filling them first before it overflows into higher ground. Of course wind can alter this flow very much and is precisely why windy Spring days are somewhat protected from sudden, unexpected frosts. Wind mixes the cold air with whatever warm air is available, thus raising the temperature of the air and reducing the chance of pockets of cold air.

One of the oldest, and still practical, ways of predicting unexpected frosts is the nighttime sky. If you are really uncertain about how low the temperature will go that night, look at the sky. If it is clear and free of clouds then you had best make plans to protect your plants. Why this is so can only be generally answered, but clear skies usually are the result of stable weather patterns. Unstable weather patterns create winds while stable ones are relatively mild. No wind means that cold air will flow to those low areas like water in a bowl. Also, clear, cloudless nights experience much more radiant cooling than cloud-covered nights. Clouds actually hold in the heat produced by daytime sunshine, resulting in less temperature drop after sundown. Clear skies let warm air quickly rise and dissipate.

You should also consider the quality and texture of the soil in which you choose to plant, although this can be remedied if deficiencies exist. Soil should be well drained and contain an abundance of organic material. pH should be slightly acid (6.5-6.8) and the texture of the loam should have equal amounts of sand, clay and humus. This is ideal soil, but finding soil like this by chance is not rare and correcting soil that is close to these characteristics can be accomplished in a season or two. In choosing a growing area for your giant pumpkin, look for full sun all day, high ground, and natural protection from wind and good soil.

*Below: Fred McDonald's wife, child and dog are camouflaged amongst the sprawling vines of his giant pumpkin patch.*

*Above: Soil preparation, for most competitive pumpkin growers, starts from manure from various farm animals.*

# Chapter 6 *Preparing the Soil*

O nce you have chosen a growing area, the task ahead revolves around an assessment of the soil and then correction of any deficiency that exists. Pumpkins are surprisingly aggressive growers but require little more than good garden soil to flourish. Large pumpkins have been grown on only marginal soil with little attention, but this is the exception to the rule and part of the persona of luck in growing a giant. Remember, the harder you work and the more knowledge you employ in growing a pumpkin, the luckier you will get.

## Testing

The first step you should take in analyzing and assessing your garden soil is to have it tested. The very minimum test should be for pH of the soil. This test and others can be performed by you with accuracy, while others should be performed by agencies or labs trained in their procedures.

## pH

A pH test can be taken in a matter of 15–20 minutes depending on the texture of the soil and the number of random tests you make. pH of soil is an important measurement to understand because it bears heavily on the availability of other major plant nutrients. pH measures the amount of hydrogen ions present in soil and as such determines whether soil is acidic or alkaline. It is reported on a measurement scale from 1–14. This scale is a logarithmic scale with each number representing a power to which 10 is raised. $10^1$ (10 to the power of 1) = 10, $10^2$ (10 to the power of 2 or 10 squared) = 100, $10^3$ (10 to the power of 3 or 10 cubed) = 1000 and so on. I present this here to show how a 1 point move in the pH scale represents 10 times as many or less hydrogen ions. A 2 point move contains 100 times more or less and a 3 point move 1000 times more or less. Soil is regarded as being neutral when its pH is 7, acid when it is below 7 and alkaline when it is above. People refer to acid soil as "sour" and alkaline soil as "sweet".

The pH of most soils will fall into a broad band around neutral (7) with some measurements reaching as low as 4 and some as high as 9. The majority of US soils will have pH test results in the 4–9 range depending on the region in which you live. Generally speaking, most of us will have soil with pH readings below 7, but some regions of the country never experience acid soils and are continually plagued by high calcium, alkaline soil with pH measurements well above 7.

In making a test of soil, you should begin with gathering a random sample of soil. It is highly unlikely that your soil pH will vary from one section of your yard to another unless you have carried on cultural improvements for many years in only one section. Within your garden area, this characteristic is even more true. It is not likely that pH will vary much within your garden area, but a random sampling is made to insure accurate results. Taking several samples (5 or 6) with a shovel to the depth of 6", and mixing them together in a wheelbarrow will guarantee that the test results represent the true soil pH.

Once mixed, make 2 or 3 tests of the sample using a test kit purchased at a local garden center. The whole testing time, including collection of the samples, will take less than half an hour, and slightly more if you test for some of the major plant nutrients present.

Pumpkins grow best in soil which has a pH range between 6.5–6.8, or soil which is slightly acid. This is a range which also suits most summertime vegetable crops and lawn grasses, so it is not surprising that pumpkins do well where tomatoes, squash, corn or grass have flourished. Following good cultural methods for your region of the country as it relates to growing tomatoes almost guarantees success with pumpkins.

In the Northeast, where I live, soil is generally very acid, sometimes having pH readings below 5-6. In almost all cases, we have to raise the pH of soil, or "sweeten" the soil with limestone. Limestone contains large quantities of calcium and sometimes magnesium. Both these elements have the ability to raise pH. They are also very important minor plant nutrients which are required by all living plants, and especially aggressive growers like pumpkins.

The reason that pH levels are so important is because all plants have some preference as to what range of pH they prefer. The pH preference range is determined by what elements are most needed by the plant. Acid loving plants like rhododendrons, azaleas and hollies require more of the minor elements of iron, sulfur and aluminum, while most vegetable crops need more calcium and magnesium. The more iron, sulfur and aluminum present the more acid the soil, and conversely, the more calcium and magnesium present, the sweeter the soil.

When we speak of pH preference ranges for certain plants, it is that range which optimizes the available plant nutrients. The expression "tied up" is often used when a plant is grown in soil which has a pH reading outside its preference range. When pumpkins are grown on soil with pH below 6 or above 7, major plant nutrients, which are present, become unavailable to its roots. In essence, the plant nutrients become tied up in the soil. The reason for this revolves around the chemistry of the soil, the attraction of elements within it and the ability of plant roots to absorb nutrients. Suffice it to say that when pH readings fall outside of the plant's range of preference, the plant will suffer from inadequate plant nutrients, even though they may be present or applied liberally before and during the growing season.

The procedures for adjusting soil pH are easily carried out with common soil additives. If your soil is too acid (with pH below 6), add limestone at the rate of 50 pounds per 1000 square feet. If your soil is too alkaline (with pH above 7), add sulfur, aluminum sulfate or copious amounts of organic matter.

The process of correcting pH may take 6 months to a year because changing the chemical properties of the soil is a slow process. In most cases, correcting pH will be rewarded in the following growing season. Test for pH 4-6 weeks after the addition of lime or sulfur to see if the pH has changed. You should see some movement towards your goal of 6.5–6.8.

## Major Plant Nutrients

The next test you should make is for the major plant nutrients. These are nitrogen, phosphorous and potassium. Their elemental symbols of N, P, and K should be recognizable to most growers because every package of fertilizer on the market bears the percentage of each of these nutrients in an N-P-K order. When we speak of a fertilizer with an analysis of 15-8-12, we are referring to a product which contains 15% nitrogen, 8% phosphorous and 12% potassium by weight. Each of these major nutrients plays a major role in plant growth and metabolism, and all are important. Each plant uses these major plant nutrients in various ratios, giving reason for why so many different formulations of fertilizer exist. To add more confusion to what to choose, the needs for each plant nutrient will change depending on the stage of life the plant is in.

## Nitrogen

Nitrogen (N) is responsible for leaf and vine development and overall green growth of the plant. Nitrogen deficiencies are detected by yellowing of leaves and slow or retarded growth. Nitrogen is highly water soluble so it has a tendency to leach from soil very quickly. The heavier your soil, the slower this leaching process. Sandy soil will lose nitrogen faster than heavy, clay loam. Since nitrogen is continuously leaching from soil, it must be added periodically throughout the growing season, or it must come from slow release sources. Most pumpkin growers today use large amounts of manure in which nitrogen is present.

Percentage of nitrogen, phosphorous and potassium from commonly used manure sources:

| | | | |
|---|---|---|---|
| Cow | .5% | .1% | .4% |
| Horse | .7% | .2% | .7% |
| Chicken | 1.5% | .7% | .4% |
| Sheep | 1.2% | .4% | .5% |

Using large amounts of manure compensates for its relatively low percentage of nutrients. Growers using manure usually speak in terms of tons or yards of manure added. A yard is equal to 27 cubic feet of material.

Nitrogen in manure is not immediately available to the plant's roots, and must go through further chemical evolution in the soil before it can be used. Explaining the process of converting nitrates to nitrites does not belong in this book, but knowing that manure contains high amounts of slow releasing nitrogen is an important fact to comprehend. Nitrogen will keep your pumpkin plant green and keep it growing at a high rate.

Be always careful of over-applying nitrogen though. Green growth could come at the expense of flower and fruit development. In the end, a balance of plant nutrients is required with nitrogen playing a major role.

## Phosphorous

Phosphorous is responsible for flower and root development as well as aiding in the plant's fight against disease. Phosphorous, the middle initial in the N-P-K breakdown, reacts much differently in the soil than nitrogen. It has a tendency to stay in the soil, and does not leach or move as nitrogen does. This fact tells growers to mix phosphorous into the growing region of the soil rather than just spreading it on top of the soil. Manure contains much phosphorous, but growers also use chemical sources to supplement the soil. Some commonly used chemical sources are super phosphate (0-20-0), triple super phosphate (0-44-0) and water soluble formulations marketed by Stern's under the Miracle Gro label and Peters Professional Plantfoods marketed under several formulations. Formulations like 5-10-5, 0-20-0, 15-30-15 and so on are all formulations stressing phosphorous as a major element. Bone meal and rock phosphate are both good sources of organic phosphorous.

## Potassium

Potassium is responsible for many of the metabolic functions of the plant including the manufacture of sugars, but most important, it aids in the active development of carbohydrates in the fruit. Much the same as phosphorous, it tends to stay in the soil, and does not leach like nitrogen.

## Testing

Testing for the major nutrients can be accomplished with store bought testers, but I have always opted for testing done by independent labs. Most State Universities with agricultural departments have testing facilities along with many field stations which are part of the Agricultural Extension Service.

## Effects of pH on Major Plant Nutrients

Major plant nutrients can be tied up in soils having pH readings below 5 or above 8. This is why a pH test, above all, is the most important test you can make in assessing your soil. Poor pH means that most of the manure or chemical fertilizers applied to your garden plot will remain unavailable to your plants. At the very minimum, make a pH test of your soil every year, and correct any deficiency which exists. Then, and only then, make more elaborate tests of major and minor nutrients as time and interest permit. Remember that knowing what to apply to your soil can never really be determined until you know what it contains. Start any soil preparation program with a good test.

*Right: Several pumpkins call this manure pile home. The combined weight easily tops 1000 pounds. Manure forms the backbone of all competitive pumpkin growers' soil building programs.*

## Applying Organic Materials to the Soil

This section addresses the practice of applying organic (once living) materials to the soil. Organic material can come from manure, compost, garden refuse, hair, seaweed and many other sources. Manure is the material of choice by growers because of its availability and relatively high plant nutrient levels. Some growers apply as much as 5 yards of manure per plant each year. This may be overkill in the fight against nutrient deficiencies, but it does insure that major plant nutrients are adequate for the plant. It also insures that organic material is present in all growing regions of the soil. Organic material keeps the soil "open" and contributes to good drainage while it conversely serves as a reservoir of air, water and plant nutrients. As organic materials decay, they are reduced to a valuable component of the soil — humus. Humus is the most important part of all loam soils and it is this ingredient that gives life to soil — holding moisture and slowly releasing important elements used by all plants.

Building up the level of humus in your soil is accomplished by adding large amounts of organic material over a period of several years. Most avid gardeners pursue this practice with a vengeance. Their attitude is that there is never too much organic matter in soil. Pumpkin growers wishing to grow larger pumpkins should learn something from these gardeners.

The downside of organic material addition is its effect on soil pH. The breakdown of organic material will create acid conditions in the soil which results in lower pH readings. Any practice of applying large quantities of organic material should be combined with the addition of limestone as an agent in equalizing these effects.,

I have found Fall to be the better time of the year to add organic material to the soil. You will have more available time and more materials to choose from. Compost made during the Summer, garden refuse, fallen leaves, and such, all become readily available for use in the Fall.

## Cover Crops

Cover crops or "green manure" also have a place in any soil preparation program. Most cover crops are seeded in the Fall with Winter Rye receiving the most use. Winter Rye is an amazingly tough grass that when given a foothold in your garden will flourish and grow under the most severe conditions. In the dead of Winter when a 40-50 degree heat wave strikes for 2-3 days, winter rye will green up and show signs of growth. It is usually seeded in the Fall and will germinate in less than a week if adequate soil moisture is present. In early Spring, a foot or more of growth can be tilled or dug into the soil. Waiting any longer can make the task of plowing under considerably more difficult. This dug in grass does wonders for the soil. Not only does it add organic material to the soil, but its very nature aids in opening up soil to air and moisture. Cover crops can also be sown in the Spring and Summer on vacant plots in which you wish to add organic material. Depending on the length of vacancy, good choices could be alfalfa, vetch, buckwheat, annual grasses, beans or peas.

## Minor Plant Nutrients

Minor plant nutrients are needed in far less quantities than major nutrients, but never-the-less, deficiencies in any one of them can have adverse effects on the growing of plants like pumpkins. Some of the more important minor nutrients to be concerned with are calcium, magnesium, manganese, iron, copper, boron, zinc and others. All play some vital role in plant growth and metabolism.

## Calcium

Calcium serves plant growth by neutralizing toxic acids which are the result of normal plant cell functions. It also acts to balance the effect of magnesium in the soil. Common soil additives like limestone contain calcium, and as such are a good source. Poultry manure is also a good source of calcium. When the effects of limestone are not wanted (higher pH), other sources like garden gypsum can be used.

## Magnesium

Magnesium is vital in the formation of chlorophyll; it is therefore essential to growth. Magnesium, present in dolomitic limestone and other sources has much the same effect on pH as does calcium. Magnesium deficient soils will show poor plant color and poor or underdeveloped flowers and fruit. Iron is also integral to the formation of chlorophyll, and therefore, is also a vital minor nutrient.

## Other Minor Nutrients

Besides calcium, magnesium and iron, manganese, copper, zinc, boron and other minor or trace elements are needed for growth of plants. Because these elements are needed in such small amounts and normal soils contain more than adequate amounts, deficiencies of them are rarely encountered.

## Special Hill Preparations

In addition to preparing the overall soil of your garden area, special considerations should be made in preparing the area in the immediate vicinity of the newly planted seedlings. Pumpkins are generally planted in "hills". This expression is used to describe, not only the technique employed for hundreds of years of planting in raised soil, but also the practice of planting more than one seed or seedling in the same area.

The practice of mounding soil slightly, thus creating a hill, has been used for centuries by growers from all over the world. The most obvious benefit comes from the fact that raised soil heats up faster than soil at normal ground level. During a warm Spring day, soil temperatures can be as much as ten degrees higher in raised beds and hills than in normal elevation soil. This aids in seed germination and also in overall growth. Remember, pumpkins are heat lovers, showing their most robust growth only after warm Summer days have arrived. Any additional soil heat in Spring will benefit them. Hills also create better air and water drainage in the soil. The physical act of preparing the hill loosens the soil and allows more air to enter. The fact that hills are raised mounds of soil also aids in draining excess moisture away from the planting area.

"Hill" is also used as a term for planting more than one seed or seedling in a location. When planting squash, pumpkins, cucumbers, melons and occasionally corn, seed is sometimes planted in groups of 3-5 plants. This practice is called hill planting regardless of the level of the soil. It is called a hill even if no mound of soil exists.

All and all, hill preparations can benefit pumpkin growers because it is one of the few preparations of soil that can accomplish increased soil temperature and better drainage. Obviously, plastic mulches and soil heating cables can be employed by growers to enhance the benefits that hill planting grants.

When preparing hills for pumpkins, some growers use additional organic material in the form of manure or compost to further improve the soil of the hill. Additional organic material and plant nutrients insures that seed and seedlings will get off to a good start. Pumpkin hills should be constructed in a way that soil is elevated about 1 foot and gradually diminishes over an area approximately 8-10' in diameter. This area is the nursery for your plants — the starting of a new season. Everything that you know about growing should be employed in this small area to insure a good start for your plants. Soil preparation, wind and frost protection and all forms of insect and disease control, weed and grass control, and varmint control should be addressed. I will cover all of these topics in detail as we proceed through the balance of this book.

# Chapter 7 Seed Starting

There are not many other areas of discussion which are more controversial among competitive pumpkin growers than seed starting. Every successful grower seems to have his/her unique way of starting seed, with each expounding its benefits. In essence, seed starting can be generally categorized into two approaches. You can either start seed indirectly by germinating them indoors or in a protected area outdoors and later transplanting them to the growing area, or you can direct seed into the final growing place. There are advantages and disadvantages for both approaches. Both approaches have seen great successes, and both have experienced devastating losses. What approach you use will be dependent on the amount of time and level of interest you have in growing giant pumpkins.

I once spoke with a retired, 79-year-old pumpkin grower, Bill Behuniak of Kingston, New York, who knew, to the minute, when each of his pumpkin seeds germinated each year. Bill is a very successful grower and a real gentleman, but few of us have the time he spends nurturing his plants into their early stages of growth. Bill theorizes that newly emerging seedlings display characteristics which continue throughout their entire life. He is acutely observant of which seedlings display the most robust and aggressive growth, and which are either slow to germinate or lacking in vigor.

*Above: A dime helps to show the true scale and size of some Dill's Atlantic Giant Pumpkin Seeds.*
*Below: A peat pot bearing a freshly emerged Atlantic Giant. Notice that the seed coating is still adhering to the seed leaves.*

Other growers strongly believe that starting seed early is wasteful, and only the hot weather of mid-Summer triggers the explosive growth which is the hallmark of giant pumpkins. They theorize that by July 15th, the race among plants, either started early or direct seeded later, is a dead heat. They contend that direct seeded plants catch up to the earlier started seeds, and they remind us of the fact that they did not take the chance of exposing seedlings to a variety of natural conditions which could have abruptly ended the seedling's life. Wind, insects, unexpected frosts, generally cool weather and the like are all hindrances to the growth of newly transplanted seedlings.

So, what is the best method? Let's look at the strengths and weaknesses of both approaches, then I leave it up to you to decide which approach makes the most sense.

## Indirect Seeding

Indirect seeding is the germination of seed in locations other than their final growing area. It normally takes place indoors, but can be accomplished outdoors with the use of cold frames, heating cables, or greenhouses. Most growers start by germinating seed in small containers for transplanting later into the garden. Most use peat pots (around 4" in diameter) filled with a light, sterilized planting mixture. These planting mixtures, or media, can be purchased at local garden centers, and most contain varying

Top: *Newly planted seedling showing only seed leaves.*
Middle: *Sprouting seed naked is practiced by many growers. Here the red coating on the seed is the result of a liberal dusting with a fungicide.*
Bottom: *New seedling with 3 true leaves.*

amounts of sphagnum peat moss, vermiculite, perlite, wool and other organic and inorganic materials. The chief characteristics of these materials is that they are very light, they hold moisture very well and they are free from harmful soil organisms. They remain fluffy even when totally saturated with water, and drain easily if there is space for excessive moisture to recede.

Seeds should be planted approximately 1–1.5" down with the pointed end of the seed facing down. This assists the seedling in pushing through the media. The seed leaves are attached to the outer covering of the seed, so the whole seed generally emerges from the soil. As the seed leaves unfurl, the seed coverings fall off. Since the first roots emerge from the pointed end of the seed, it is only logical that the seed be positioned in the soil so that the roots are facing down and the leaves are facing upward.

Newly planted seeds should be placed in a warm area, such as the top of a refrigerator. Some growers choose to use heating cables placed at the base of their peat pots to insure even warmth. The ideal germination temperature is between 75-85 degrees. When this range is obtained, germination will occur in 3 days or less. The new seed literally explodes from the media, pushing up its seed leaves, as it struggles to open to the light. This is an exciting time for a grower because it marks the beginning of the new growing season and the start of a plant that could very well be the next world champion.

Some growers carry the indirect seeding method through an additional step by first germinating their seeds "naked". Instead of germinating their seeds in peat pots, they germinate their seed in paper towels, on sponges or on other wet environments where they can observe, totally, the beginning of growth. After germination has occurred, they gingerly transplant these small seedlings to their temporary peat-pot homes.

Soon after the seed leaves open, new leaves begin to sprout from the seed leaf axils. These are the first true leaves of the pumpkin plant, and their emergence marks a critical stage for growers using an indirect seeding method. Pumpkins are easily harmed by movement at this early stage of development yet prolonging transplanting puts them in even greater danger. Any disruption of their roots can cause a quick death. So, it is important to not delay transplanting to the final growing area once true leaves have opened.

## Light, Moisture and Ventilation

Seedlings should be exposed to as much light as possible after emergence. Growing inside almost always requires additional light sources. Erecting a shop light fixture with fluorescent tubes over your plants is probably the best way to provide additional light. Some manufacturers produce fluorescent tubes with corrected light waves which more closely resemble natural sunlight, although normal tubes are adequate for our use. These lights should be placed so that seedlings are no more than 6" away from the tubes. You may have to adjust your fixture, or pot placement as growth proceeds. Since the plants will be indoors for only 2-3 weeks, this is not a big inconvenience.

In addition, moisture levels and air ventilation are important considerations during these early stages of growth. Pumpkin plants are very sensitive to diseases when grown in overly moist media or in low ventilation environments where humidity is high. Never water directly onto your seedlings and never cover them with plastic to increase humidity in the growing area. Most growers take an additional precaution by treating their seeds with Captan (a commonly available fungicide). This helps to combat disease, rotting of seeds and damping off of seedlings.

These precautions also apply to the area in which you finally transplant your seedlings. If you choose to plant in a protective enclosure, make sure that there is adequate light and moisture and good ventilation.

## Roots of New Seedlings

If you carefully observe your seedlings, you will see that root growth is almost as rapid as leaf growth. In two weeks, roots will already be making their way throughout the initial starting media, and may begin to show at the bottom of the peat pots. These roots are very sensitive to any movement, and not handling them with care will result in very poor transplanting results. The reason why growers prefer peat pots over plastic or terra cotta pots is because they know they can transplant the seedling, pot and all, when the time comes. Trying to remove a seedling from a pot at this stage of life will almost always lead to failure.

The advantages to starting seed indirectly are many, but the key ones are: the ability to control and monitor the early stages of growth, and the ability to start seed before the last frost date has been reached.

## Early Control

Planting indirectly allows a grower the pleasure and control of intense scrutiny of his seedlings. If the right conditions of temperature and moisture are obtained, germination is fairly predictable. After germination, a grower has the ability to completely shield the young seedling from any natural occurrence or life threatening exposure. Protection from frost, extreme drought and varmints such as woodchucks are all but eliminated at this early stage. This control must be eventually compromised when plants are transplanted outside, but for these early stages, nothing beats the security of planting indoors.

## Earlier Starting Dates

Planting indirectly allows planting prior to the average last frost date. As you already know, pumpkin seedlings will not tolerate any exposure to frost. Starting indoors gives initial protection from freezing temperatures and allows a grower to start seeds 2-3 weeks ahead of expected last frost dates. Every region of the country has an average last frost date, but this date can vary dramatically within a region and from year to year. Isolated frosts can occur unexpectedly almost anywhere where people rely on average last frost dates as their rule of planting. Your yard may even experience an isolated frost in one location while others only several yards away escape.

It is critical that seedlings be planted before extensive root growth has occurred. This is why 2-3 weeks is the maximum time to allow for holding plants indoors. You will want a small but vigorous seedling to transplant outside after danger of frost has passed. 2-3 weeks is ample time, under controlled conditions to produce a good candidate for your garden.

*Right: A minigreenhouse serves to protect newly planted seedlings from frost and wind while elevating daytime temperatures slightly. Below: Howard Dill direct seeds into a mini greenhouse structure in the growing area.*

Along with controls granted with indirect seeding comes the added responsibility of careful transplanting. New seedlings, grown exclusively indoors, are very tender. The term "harden off" is often used for the procedures used in acclimating a new seedling to outside weather conditions. Slowly allowing more exposure to fluctuating heat, wind and soil moisture should take place over a period of several days. Some growers choose to use cold frames which they can adjust to allow exposure to increased temperatures and more rapid air movement. They can be easily constructed using an old storm window and creative use of materials you already have. I have seen them constructed using bales of straw, pallets wrapped in plastic and other exotic designs. They all serve the purpose of protecting the seedlings from extreme cold, yet exposing them to more sunlight, higher temperatures and more natural growing conditions. Cold frames must be constructed in a way that allows the grower the ability to adjust the amount of air entering and leaving the structure. A simple sash on hinges solves this problem in many cases.

Other growers plant their seedlings directly in their final growing area, and then erect protective structures over them. Both methods work admirably with planting in the garden having a slight edge. Remember, seedlings can only be held so long in a cold frame before transplanting becomes a dangerous undertaking. I will cover theses protective enclosures in more detail in Chapter 10 Plant Protection.

## Direct Seeding

Direct seeding is the germination of seed in its final growing area. The distinct advantage of direct seeding over indirect is that new seedlings do not have to be transplanted and moved. Many growers contend that trans-

planting, no matter how cautious it is undertaken, stresses the new seedling and slows the momentum of growth.

Planting and germinating seed outdoors requires the same steps taken in planting and germinating indoors. The seed is planted in the same way, and some growers prepare the general area with sterilized seed starting media. The lighter mixture helps in the initial stages of germination. It also lowers the chances of diseases associated with damping off.

Most growers using the direct seed method contend that 2-3 weeks lost using their method of seed starting does not really effect the plant's overall growth. The argument that pumpkins are heat lovers justifies their position on choosing to plant later. New seedlings subjected to cool weather lose their momentum of growth. Stress to prematurely set transplants is enough to eliminate gains obtained from early indirect seeding. If you get a number of sub 50 degree nights after transplanting a new seedling, you will probably lose any time gained in lengthening the growing season.

Direct seeding should occur when soil is warm. Remember that the ideal temperature for pumpkin seed germination is 75-85 degrees. It will take an extremely warm day in early May to accomplish this in New England. Late May or early June has better conditions where I live, even though the average last frost date is May 15th. Growers who expound the advantages of direct seeding will invariably use the argument (and justifiably) that pumpkin plants do not grow well when nighttime temperatures dip into the 50's and high 40's. In late Spring in New England, we are continually subjected to these conditions, so it is far better to wait to plant than to set out plants in unfavorable conditions.

## Beating Mother Nature

There are common methods and practices employed by both indirect seeded and direct seeded growers which revolve around the use of heating cables, temporary protective structures and a lot of nighttime precaution. Many growers erect what constitutes greenhouses over their young plants. These are built to protect the young plant as well as improving the growing conditions. These protective shelters elevate soil temperature and protect plants from moderate frosts and buffeting winds.

Although these methods are very successful, they rely on a much higher level of commitment from the grower. You can still grow a giant pumpkin by planting much later and avoiding early cold weather, but truly competitive pumpkin growers will go to any length to extend the growing season in hopes that it will result in a larger pumpkin. No evidence suggests that early planting benefits pumpkin size, but many top growers exploit early planting and suggest that it is the very reason for their success.

Whether you choose to seed indirectly or directly will be based on your commitment to growing a giant pumpkin and the time you have available. There are successful growers using both methods. You can be successful using any one of the methods as long as you cater to the needs of your plants.

*Above: George Brooks' direct seeding method shows good germination and produces a big jump start for the growing season.*
*Below: A hilled mound complete with a soil heating cable and cover is the hallmark of Brook's innovative direct seeding method.*

# Chapter 8 *Planting and Spacing*

There are not too many things to remember about planting either seed or transplants of pumpkins other than the obvious. Pumpkins require a lot of space, so plants cannot be over-crowded in small garden plots. Many growers, lacking more space, plant pumpkins in areas less than 300 square feet (15' x 20') with moderate success. But, most growers agree that the more space allocated for each plant, the better. Standard recommendations for spacing giant pumpkins range from 25–45' between plants, making a single planting area 625 square feet (25' x 25') to 2025 square feet (45' x 45'). The rule of thumb used by most growers is 1000 square feet per plant, or approximately 33' between plants.

If you decided to grow 3 plants, you will need a garden area of about 30' x 100". I do not have this kind of space myself, so I raise only 2 plants per year. Many, fine successful growers get by with growing 3 or less plants per season. You can see that growing small numbers of plants per year puts a heavy emphasis on choosing the right seed.

Your growing area should be well cultivated and thoroughly prepared before planting. Reading Chapter 6, Preparing the Soil and Chapter 11, Fertilizing and Watering will help you to decide what is appropriate. You should also have protective screens or enclosures in place to insure that wind or unexpected frosts do not damage your new seedlings. These protective devices can be as simple as a Hot Kap™ or modified milk carton at first, but as the plant grows, more elaborate precautions should be taken. You will learn more on this subject in Chapter 10, Plant Protection.

You begin by direct seeding or transplanting your seedlings to a thoroughly prepared hill. You should expect losses from both methods (indirect or direct seeding) and as a result, should plan on planting several candidates in each hill. If you plant 5 seeds or seedlings per hill, you should mark the locations of each if they come from different pumpkins. It is important to know who your plant's parents are so that you can make a better evaluation of the plant at the end of the season. In most cases, you will know the mother of your seed or seedling if you buy non–certified seed, or are given seed from another grower. The seed is simply named for the weight of the pumpkin that produced it. If you are lucky enough to grow a real monster pumpkin, knowing as much about its lineage as possible will help in duplicating this achievement in future seasons.

Some growers plant as many as 10 seeds per hill to start, choosing to wait until the seedlings have matured to the 5–7 leaf stage before beginning culling. The reason for planting so many seeds or seedlings per hill to start is because germinating and nurturing pumpkin seedlings is risky business. You will undoubtedly lose plants to poor germination (they never emerge from the soil), unexpected frosts, insect and varmint invasions and anything else that could happen. It's the old Murphy's Law. If something bad can happen to your seeds or seedlings, it probably will.

Planting 5–10 seeds or seedlings per hill is a numbers game. If you plant enough seed, you probably will have a few good seedlings to choose from when the time comes for final culling. Most growers choose to cull slowly over a period of 3–4 weeks — eliminating obvious runts and damaged plants at first, and then isolating the most vigorous plant.

When making the decision over which plants to keep and which to cull, you should consider the lineage of each seedling. If two seedlings have identical vitality, then the seedling with the best lineage should be chosen as the final plant. If lineage is not known, or the seeds came from the same pumpkin, then your decision is a game of chance. This is where luck enters the equation for success. Two seedlings may look remarkably alike at this stage, but produce dramatically different results in pumpkin weights. I hope you are lucky when making your final decision on which seedling to keep and which to cull.

Each hill should contain one plant when final culling is complete—and this plant should be spaced 25–45' from its nearest neighbor if space permits. These "anointed ones" should get the red carpet treatment. Start by feeding them a good, water soluble starter fertilizer. Most of these will contain ratios with emphasis placed on phosphorous; therefore, 15-30-15, 10-20-10, or the like, should be used at this time. This practice should be adopted, over and above other soil preparation and fertilizer program plans. Treating with high phosphorous water soluble fertilizers should occur about once a week for the first month, applying liberally to the area occupied by the young plant. This will insure good initial root growth. After 3-4 weeks, other fertilizer strategies will be used. You will learn more on this subject in Chapter 11, Fertilizing and Watering.

*Left: Don Fleming spaces plants amply to allow for their aggressive growth behavior.*

# Chapter Nine *Pumpkin Growth Stages*

If you look at the information contained on seed packages or read some horticultural references, you will find that it takes between 120-150 days to grow an Atlantic Giant Pumpkin. In case you do not realize it, that is 4-5 months. If you live in a climate such as New England, the northern United States, southern Canada, or at high altitude, you begin to notice that squeezing 120-150 frost-free days out of your Spring, Summer and Fall may not be possible, or at the very least, risky. It behooves a grower living in a region that borders on 120 frost-free days to maximize each and every day during this time period. This means being attentive to your plant and the weather, planning and taking preventative measures. It also means taking the appropriate action at the appropriate time in the life of the pumpkin plant.

There are special practices which successful growers perform at specific times in the life of the pumpkin plant which spell the difference between a large and a giant pumpkin. These practices fall into general categories which are related to the stage of life in which the pumpkin is in. Knowing these growth stages will help you to isolate what is important at that time, and what practices should take priority over others. When looking at the life cycle of a pumpkin, we can define 3 distinct stages of growth which all require unique cultural practices. These 3 stages can be summarized into the seedlings growth stage, leaf and root growth stage and finally, the fruit growth stage. Obviously, your pumpkin must progress through all these stages on its way to the end of the season, but knowing approximately when each stage begins and ends will help you to recognize when it is appropriate for you to shift gears, and begin treating your pumpkin based on its most important needs.

## Seedling Growth Stage

The seedling growth stage lasts 10–14 days under ideal conditions of temperature and sunlight. If soil temperatures reach 75–85 degrees, seeds will germinate in 3–5 days. The end of this growth stage is marked by the appearance of three fully developed true leaves. This takes about 2–3 weeks after seedlings emerge from the soil. The priorities during this stage of life are soil or media warmth. The warmth can be provided by soil heating cables, indoor devices or Mother Nature, but it must occur at the right time and at the right amount. Seeds left in cool, moist soil for too long will likely rot, even if treated with a general fungicide like Captan or sulfur. Once seed has germinated and emerged, the next priority is sunlight, maintenance of soil warmth and protection from wind and frost. If you indirectly seed indoors, these priorities have already been addressed. If you seed directly into the final growing area, you must provide temporary protection. This temporary protection, at first, can be little more than a plastic milk carton with the bottom cut off. This and similar, homemade devices act like mini-greenhouses. The precautions of using these devices are related to overheating during the day and less than full protection at night. You may have to remove the device on a 60–70 degree day, but cover it up on a night in which you expect a frost. You can cover it with any insulating material such as a blanket, canvas, straw or the like. More elaborate precautions can be made by constructing cold frames over the newly emerging seedlings and providing bottom heat from soil heating cables. Covering these shelters is also advised on cold nights. Some growers build small shelters measuring about 16 square feet (4'x4') and incorporate ways to adjust air flow and temperature for times when overheating can occur. The key priorities during the seedling growth stage are warmth and protection. If you concentrate on these for the first 14–21 days of your pumpkin's life, you will be doing everything you can do to insure its vitality.

## Leaf and Root Growth Stage

The next stage is characterized by rapid growth of the plant with main vines, secondary vines and roots growing at amazing rates. Growth can be as much as 6" to a foot per day This growth stage sees three changes in the feeding strategy which closely follow the needs of the plant. During the early part of this stage, emphasis should be placed on providing phosphorous for root growth, gradually shifting to more balanced formulations with more nitrogen for green growth of the plant, culminating in a switch to a higher potassium formulation for development of the set fruit. This all occurs in 60–70 days starting with 3 true leaves and ending with the desired fruit set. Fruit set refers to a pollinated fruit which meets your standards of quality and will be left on the vine to fully mature. Generally speaking, the chosen fruit will have been on the vine for 2–3 weeks before final selection is made. Leaving others on the vine for longer periods does insure that you will have more than one pumpkin to choose from should disaster strike the most likely candidate. After 4–5 weeks, you should cull all but the chosen fruits. There are pumpkin growers who grow more than one pumpkin on their plants. I will cover the pros and cons of single or multiple fruit later in this book in Chapter 16, Pruning and Pinching. During this stage, an amazing amount of root growth will occur.

## Fruit Growth Stage

The fruit growth stage lasts between 70–80 days. It starts with fruit set and ends when the pumpkin is harvested. During this period of time the Atlantic Giant pumpkin will increase in weight from a few ounces at fruit-set to several hundred pounds at harvest. Additions to weight during the peak of this stage can be as much as 25 pounds per day. This tremendous growth can lead to many problems which I will explore in detail later.

A common way of estimating pumpkin weight is by measurement of the circumference of the fruit at the widest point. I will discuss measurement techniques in Chapter 18, Measuring for Approximate Weight, but for now you should know that a pumpkin can increase 5–6" per day in total circumference during early stages of growth. This amazing growth can only hap-

pen if good weather conditions, adequate moisture and sufficient plant nutrients exist. Howard Dill sums it up nicely in a descriptive note accompanying his seed orders,

> *"For those growing the "really big ones" the most important things to remember are seeds, soil, sunshine and moisture."*

Wayne Hackney explains in his paper, *The Law of Limiting Factors* that a pumpkin's growth is limited by deficiencies in any of the factors of its growth. He explains that sunlight, water temperature and fertilizer are the most important factors to be aware of, but

> *"There are literally dozens and dozens of factors that affect plant growth and every one  must be optimized to get a record breaker"*

During the fruit growth stage, you must seek to optimize the effects of anything which affects plant growth and seek to discover deficiencies which limit growth and then correct them. We cannot always just concentrate on the most obvious factors such as fertilizer and moisture, and we cannot always be in control as it relates to many factors such as sunshine and temperature. Luck enters again. The optimally grown pumpkin will be a joint effort between Mother Nature (seed, sunlight, temperature and moisture) and the grower (seed, soil fertilizer and moisture).

We cannot always expect seed to act as we plan. Mother Nature occasionally modifies genes, or holds little surprises that we never expect. We can however improve our chances of growing the really big one by seeking out the best seed that is available. We can only seek to improve our chances—Mother Nature is in control of the results. Sunlight and temperature, except for some devices used by growers in the seedling stage, is completely controlled by Mother Nature. On a 40 degree night in July, we can do little, but sit and pray that the effects of cold will not do irreparable damage. We can provide the necessary moisture by manual means to sustain the biggest pumpkin. Mother Nature helps, but occasionally gets carried away with a surplus of moisture which batters leaves, slows growth and creates an environment conducive to the spread of disease. The only real control we have is in the preparation of the soil and fertilizer applied to the growing area.

During the fruit growth stage we must be keenly aware that the needs of the plant have begun to change from nutrients for leaf and vine growth to nutrients for development of fruit. Since a pumpkin is simply a seed and carbohydrate storage area on the vine, it is only logical that plant nutrients which enhance carbohydrate development should be present in the soil, or increased in the feeding program. During the fruit growth stage growers often switch from balanced fertilizer formulations (used in the leaf and root growth stage) to formulations which contain a higher percentage of potassium. Potassium is chiefly responsible for carbohydrate formation. It is needed in all stages of life for the pumpkin, but never more than during the fruit growth stage. If you choose to use water soluble fertilizers, a switch to a 1-1-2 or 1-1-3 ratio is advised to optimize growth. Most water soluble formulations also contain many of the minerals and trace elements needed

*Left Page*
   *Top: George Brook's newly set pumpkin on July 3rd.*
   *Middle: July 16th.*
   *Bottom: July 27th.*
*Right Page*
   *Above: August 5th.*

by all plants. Although they are needed in only small amounts, anyone of them can limit the growth of your pumpkin if they are deficient. Using water solubles which also contain calcium, magnesium, iron, zinc, manganese and more can only help your chances of combating any limiting factors of growth.

Limiting factors caused from insects, disease, wind, hail, and the like can sometimes be controlled, and sometimes not at all. As a world-class giant pumpkin grower, you can only try to increase your chances of growing a truly giant pumpkin; Mother Nature has the final say in the results.

The key priorities of the fruit growth stage are increased awareness of deficiencies and any limiting factors of growth, and increased emphasis of potassium and minor elements for optimal fruit growth.

## Summary

Cater to the needs of your pumpkin plants as their growth stages dictate. If you follow this practice, you will be half way towards optimizing the conditions for your plants.

*Above: Early season planting means being especially cautious with overnight protection. Here, hills are covered with blankets and other insulating materials to reduce the chances of frost damage.*
*Right: Protective enclosures in the Fall can extend the growing season for a particularly promising pumpkin.*
*Below: Plastic covered mini greenhouses can spell the difference between saving or losing tender plants in the early season*

# Chapter 10 Plant Protection

In this chapter we will cover those aspects of plant protection which are not covered more specifically in Chapters 12, 13, 14 and 17. We will not dwell for very long on specific topics such as insect or varmint control here. This chapter is, however, an important part of this book because it concentrates on protective measures you can take against some of the forces of Nature, and ways in which you can alleviate the stress on a pumpkin plant that is growing at an enormous rate. Atlantic Giant Pumpkins grow so fast that they can literally tear themselves apart. Knowing how to position vines and pumpkins, along with some removal of anchor roots, can greatly alleviate stress on the pumpkin's stem, and hopefully keep your pumpkin growing right up until harvest.

Protecting your plant against early and late season cold weather, frosts and winds will be discussed in this chapter. Most of the practices mentioned here have been universally adopted by most top competitive pumpkin growers. Although there is argument over methods, all successful giant pumpkin growers agree that pumpkins must be protected against wind, frost and their own aggressive growth behavior.

## Wind and Frost

Wind and frost are the two biggest enemies of pumpkin plants. Even though the Atlantic Giant pumpkin is a huge specimen, with extremely aggressive growth habits, it still remains a very tender annual plant. It is so tender that the slightest frost can end the season, and the slightest wind can ripple through its giant leaves leaving a wake of damage.

Most good vegetable growers know the approximate date of their last expected Spring frost. Most smart growers also know that relying on an average or approximate date as being secure from frost is foolhardy, and will eventually lead to unexpected disaster. Most of us will want to get a jump on the season by planting before the average last frost date in hopes of extending the season. This practice, however, must be accompanied by protective measures which are carried out well before and after expected cold weather. The best way to protect early planted seedlings is to provide shelter for them from wind and temperatures that occur unexpectedly. This early protection can be as simple as a plastic milk container with its bottom removed. This crude device can serve to create greenhouse-like conditions for your new seedling, but will rapidly lose its effectiveness as the plant grows. Since all pumpkins grow quickly, some device must be erected to cover the plants well into the growing season. Obviously, if you plant in warm soil, well after the last expected Spring frost date, these measures will not be necessary, but if you require an early start because of a short grow-ing season, you will have to address cold weather from the very beginning. Erecting a small, light, portable cold frame over each hill is the best way to provide protection from frost and wind. A structure made from scrap lum-ber, strapping or other materials around your home can serve very well. You can cover the structure with either clear plastic or floating row cover material (Remay™). Both will clearly reduce wind damage and elevate soil and air temperatures. It is important that you either remove the cold frame on warm days or incorporate doors into your design so that air circulation can be provided to reduce temperatures. 4' x 4' seems to be the best size because it is large enough to provide several weeks of growing protection, yet small enough to be mobile and easily handled. It does not have to be elaborate. A structure resembling a box (4' x 4' x 2') is more than adequate. Your creativity may lead to a more practical or less costly structure. I have seen growers use old storm windows and doors and an assortment of household refuse to create effective cold frames.

Above: Alan Nesbitt pulls back the protective covering to examine one of his late season giant squash.

Some growers will also use soil heating cables under their new seedlings to further protect them from cold weather. Soil cables can easily elevate soil temperature in the root zone by up to 10 degrees; however, they are expen-sive to buy and operate, and you must have a source of electricity nearby.

Another ingenious method is the use of the "hot bed" principle. This requires a lot more work, but replicates a practice carried on for hundreds of years. You will need fresh manure, not always available to everyone, and time for preparation. In essence, you will be creating a compost pile beneath the ground's surface. Your prepared hill and protective structure rest above it. You first start by digging a 4' x 4' x 3' hole, carefully remov-ing soil so as to not mix any of the top soil with the underlying subsoil. Then you fill the hole with 2.5' of a mixture of fresh manure and leaves. Cover this with 6" of top soil, and then prepare your hill as you would ordi-narily. As the manure composts the leaves, tremendous amounts of heat will be generated. This will more than adequately heat the soil for 2–3 weeks, and get you through some very severe cold spells.

Of course, regardless of the method you use, with or without soil heating devices, cold frame structures should be covered on cold nights. A canvas or blanket could spell the difference between life and death on a below freezing night.

When your seedlings have outgrown their 4' x 4' structure, you will be well into the growing season, and well beyond any frosts. Once you remove this temporary protection, you should start protective practices which shelter the entire growing area from wind. A fence around your garden made from inexpensive conservation fence, snow fence or natural screens are the best solutions. Mark Woodward of Leominster, Massachusetts uses 4' x 8' pieces of plywood attached to 8' steel u-posts with drywall screws. We are not all blessed with natural screens, but if you have them in your yard, and they allow you to plant your pumpkin patch near them, they can provide a lot of protection for your plants. A tall row of evergreens to the North and Northeast of your patch can provide an ideal growing area for your pumpkins. You still must have good exposure to sun and good soil or use of these areas is not practical.

*Above: Vine anchoring with 18" bamboo stick criss-crossed over the vine can secure the plant from the ravages of wind.*
*Below: Coat hangers, cut and shaped into innovative vine anchors, shows that your house is full of useful gardening accessories if you are creative.*

## Vine Anchoring

Another practical way for protecting your plants from wind is the practice of anchoring vines. Anchoring vines prevents movement of the vine and reduces damage to anchor roots which occur along the vine at every leaf. There are a number of ways in which this can be done. Your own ingenuity and the materials you have on hand will dictate what course you take. One method uses 18" bamboo stakes, criss-crossed into the ground over the vine, while another method uses bent coat hangers fashioned into neat u-shaped hold-downs. After 2–3 weeks of root growth, these anchors can be removed and used further out on the vine where new growth and roots are beginning to develop. Some growers will also cover the vines with soil as these anchors are removed, giving additional support for the vine.

## Vine Positioning

Managing the direction in which your main and secondary vines grow should also be an important preoccupation. Positioning vines will make for a better use of the growing area and reduce the stress on the pumpkins contained in them.

I will more thoroughly cover which fruit to grow on to the end of the season in Chapter 15, Pollination and Fruit Setting. For now, know that you should look for one which has a wide angle on the vine. This, almost perpendicular to the vine, position will help to discourage stem stress later. As the pumpkin grows, its shoulders will extend forward, many times touching the vine to which it is attached. With the vine anchored to the

*Left: Late season special protection for prized specimens can consist of greenhouse-like structures such as this.*

ground by anchor roots on either side of the pumpkin fruit, and the position of the stem ever rising because of the enlargement of the fruit, an enormous amount of stress is inflicted on the stem. The stem does not appreciably elongate during this period of rapid pumpkin growth so, something has to give. In most cases, the stem breaks from the pumpkin ending all hopes of continued growth. Positioning vines early so that they grow

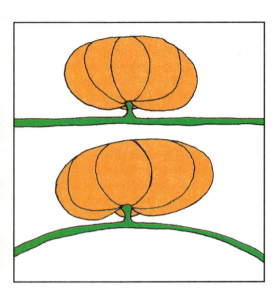

*Above: Vine training can prevent pumpkin shoulders from coming in contact with the vine, and prevent stress on the fragile stem. The bottom vine has been trained to grow away from the pumpkin's shoulders, thus reducing the chances of stem stress.*
*Below: The "S" curve of the vine, referred to in the text, puts the pumpkin in the best position to handle stem and shoulder stress. The vine on the right shows the correct position of fruit to vine.*

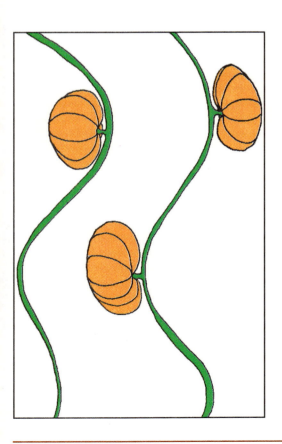

away from the pumpkin reduces the chances that the rapidly growing shoulders will extend to push the vines. Positioning your vines and pumpkin so that the pumpkin occurs on the outermost curve of a gradual "S" shape will help. The illustration on this page will help you to understand this principle more fully. This positioning should, however, be done early and gradually to insure that no stem damage occurs. This, in effect, moves the vines further away from the shoulders of the fruit, and reduces the chance of shoulder/vine stress.

In addition, secondary vines in the vicinity of the set fruit should also be trained away from the fruit. These secondary vines can restrict the movement of the pumpkin as it enlarges, and also create stem stress. It is important to understand that the pumpkin's stem does not lengthen a great deal throughout the growing season. The pumpkin will be growing at a much higher rate than the stem, and the position at which the stem attaches to the pumpkin will be continuously rising as the fruit develops. If the vines cannot move and the stem is not lengthening, the stem is almost certainly to break from the fruit or vine.

Anything which blocks the rapid growth of the fruit will ultimately stress the stem. We will discuss severing anchor roots in Chapter 17, Pumpkin Protection.

## End of Season Protection

Getting an extra 2–4 weeks of growing time at the end of the season can mean the difference between a large pumpkin and a potential weigh-off site winner. Even late in the season, giant pumpkins can still be growing at the rate of 2-5 pound per day. Keeping them growing also means that they are not losing weight. Once the fruit stops increasing in size, a ripening of the fruit begins. As the pumpkin ripens it gradually loses water through dissipation. A pumpkin can easily lose 1 pound a day after being severed from the vine, and most top growers believe that the pumpkin begins losing weight as soon as it stops increasing in size. If your pumpkin begins to ripen in early September, chances are that it will weigh less at your October weigh-off.

Most growers, suspecting that they have an unusually large pumpkin, will erect greenhouse-like structures over their growing areas to prevent early Fall frosts from damaging their plants. These structures are made from either Remay™ (floating row cover) or clear plastic. They are costly and time consuming to erect, but they are very effective in elevating daytime temperatures and preventing damage from minor frosts. Don Fleming who grows pumpkins in Northern Vermont supports a floating row cover using 55-gallon drums and a center post modified with a plastic garbage can lid. He places the post in the center of the patch, and attaches a smooth plastic garbage can cover to the top of it. He then drapes the row cover over it and over 55-gallon drums lining the perimeter of the patch. He uses old tires placed on top of the drums to hold down the cover. The plastic lid on the center post prevents the cover from tearing. He has found that the structure can withstand 25–28 degree nighttime temperatures as long as leaves are not allowed to touch the cover. Daytime temperatures in September, under the cover, often reach between 80–90 degrees giving ideal temperatures for continued growth.

# Chapter 11 Fertilizing and Watering

This chapter could be very difficult to comprehend if we allow ourselves to be overwhelmed by the amount of fertilizer alternatives we have available. If we are to make this chapter as simple as possible to understand, fertilizer alternatives will be summarized as belonging to one of two groups: organic or chemical.

## Organic Fertilizer

Organic gardening has been with us for thousands of years. The use of farm refuse, stable manure, cover crops and slash and burn farming techniques have been practiced by just about every civilized culture. Top pumpkin growers are notorious users of organic sources of plant nutrients. Manure of all kinds is used by just about every world class grower as the basic ingredient in his soil building program. Manure adds all the major plant nutrients (N-P-K) as well as many of the minor and trace elements. It also adds valuable organic matter to the soil which eventually is broken down into humus. Manure, by percentage of weight, is very low in plant nutrients, but growers compensate for this by applying huge amounts to their garden areas. Len Stellpflug, a world class squash grower, adds as much as 5 yards of manure per pumpkin plant, spread in a 30' diameter area. 5 yards of manure could weigh several thousand pounds, so you can see where small percentages of a nutrients can add up when using these huge amounts.

There is much controversy as to what manure is best to use, although all of them have proven effective. Livestock and poultry manure have all proved their worth through the years. As top pumpkin growers go, there seems to be no definitive answer as to what to use. I can only reflect on my

*Left: Gary Keyzer, the "Midwestern Maniac", is never at a loss for comical interpretations of his organic growing methods.*

| FERTILIZER COMPARISON TABLE | | | |
|---|---|---|---|
| **Chemical Sources** | **%N** | **%P** | **%K** |
| Anhydrous ammonia | 82.0 | 0.00 | 0.00 |
| Ammonium nitrate | 34.0 | 0.00 | 0.00 |
| Ammonium sulfate | 20.5 | 0.00 | 0.00 |
| Calcium nitrate | 15.0 | 0.00 | 0.00 |
| Diammonium phosphate | 18.0 | 46.0 | 0.00 |
| Monoammonium phosphate | 11.0 | 48.0 | 0.00 |
| Nitrate of potash | 13.0 | 0.00 | 44.0 |
| Nitrate of soda-potash | 15.0 | 0.00 | 14.0 |
| | | | |
| Superphosphate | 0.00 | 20.0 | 0.00 |
| Triple superphosphate | 0.00 | 44.0 | 0.00 |
| | | | |
| Sulfate of potash-magnesia | 0.00 | 0.00 | 21.8 |
| Sulfate of potash | 0.00 | 0.00 | 50.0 |
| Muriate of potash | 0.00 | 0.00 | 60.0 |
| **Organic Sources** | | | |
| Activated sludge | 5.00 | 3.00 | 0.00 |
| Alfalfa hay | 2.45 | 0.50 | 2.10 |
| Animal tankage | 8.00 | 20.0 | 0.00 |
| Blood meal | 15.0 | 1.30 | .700 |
| Cattle manure (fresh) | .290 | .170 | .350 |
| Coffee grounds | 1.99 | .360 | .670 |
| Cornstalks | .750 | .400 | .900 |
| Cottonseed | 3.15 | 1.25 | 1.15 |
| Cottonseed meal | 0.00 | 8.70 | 24.0 |
| Dried blood | 12.0 | 3.00 | 0.00 |
| Fish scrap | 8.00 | 13.0 | 4.00 |
| Greensand | 0.00 | 0.00 | 5.00 |
| Guano | 0.00 | 1.50 | 5.00 |
| Horse manure (fresh) | .440 | .170 | .350 |
| Phosphate rock | 0.00 | 30.0 | 0.00 |
| Poultry manure (fresh) | 2.00 | 1.88 | 1.85 |
| Rabbit manure (fresh) | 2.40 | .620 | .050 |
| Seaweed | 1.68 | .750 | 5.00 |
| Sheep manure (fresh) | .550 | .310 | .150 |
| Swine manure (fresh) | .600 | .410 | .130 |
| Wood ashes | 0.00 | 1.50 | 7.00 |

*Above: This chart compares the percentage values of major plant nutrients for organic and chemical fertilizers.*

observations, and as I see it, many top growers prefer the use of poultry manure. Poultry manure is proportionately higher in nitrogen than livestock manure. This tends to support the fact that nitrogen is a very valuable plant nutrient and must be supplied slowly over long periods of time because of its habit of leaching from the soil. Organic sources of nitrogen must be broken down in the soil to a form of nitrogen that plants can use. This process helps to provide the slow feeding effects most top growers strive for.

Regardless of the source of manure, manure should be the basic ingredient in your soil building and soil fertility program. Other organic materials such as compost should also be used. In addition, more concentrated forms of organic plant nutrients exist, and many growers use these in addition to manure. Popular organic fertilizers are dried blood, cottonseed meal, rock phosphate, bone meal, greensand and more. All have importance in any organic fertilizer program and each is preferred by one grower or another. Organic sources of plant nutrients must be broken down in the soil before plant's roots can use them. This process provides a slow feed and also reduces the problems associated with over feeding. Dried blood and cottonseed meal are both used as concentrated sources of organic nitrogen, while bone meal and rock phosphate provide phosphorous and greensand provides valuable potassium, along with many other minerals.

A table is presented here to compare organic and chemical sources of plant nutrients. The numbers represent average percentages of weight. Obviously, organic fertilizers are much lower by percentage weight than chemical sources, but you can overcome these low percentages by applying more of the product.

## Chemical Fertilizers

Most top growers supplement their fertilizer programs with the use of chemical fertilizers. These products can be purchased as bagged, dry goods which can be applied directly to the soil, or as soluble powders which are mixed with water and either applied to the soil or directly to the leaves. Most chemical fertilizers contain all the major plant nutrients but in varying amounts. Most growers tend to use balanced products like 10-10-10 and 15-15-15 although there are as many different formulations as there are stars in the heavens.

My advice to the new grower is to supplement manure with balanced chemical fertilizers to fortify the soil, and use water soluble fertilizers during the growing season to enhance growth. The water solubles can be delivered through overhead sprinkler systems, drip irrigation, hand watering or spraying on leaves via a compression sprayer. Almost all the top growers use water solubles in this way. Peters Professional Plantfoods and Stern's Miracle Gro both have several formulations to choose from and all seem to deliver favorable results. Peters' 20-20-20 and Stern's Miracle Gro 15-30-15 have both been lauded by various gardeners and giant pumpkin growers. Water soluble plant food should be a part of any fertilizer program used to grow world-class giant pumpkins.

## Fertilizer Strategies

Understanding what your pumpkin plant needs at different stages of growth dictates what plant food should be used. An understanding of what major and minor plant nutrients do for growth will help you to understand why a plant needs different amounts of each plant nutrient at different stages of its growth.

## Nitrogen

Nitrogen, along with magnesium and iron, is essential in the production of chlorophyll. It is easy to deduce that when green growth is at its highest rate, these nutrients should also be amply available. During the leaf and root growth stage, which starts when a seedling has three true leaves and ends when a finalist fruit is set, nitrogen and nutrients responsible for green growth should be stressed. Emphasizing nitrogen will result in more rapid root, leaf and vine growth. During this stage of growth, it is important to get as much vine and leaf growth as possible, so a large plant will be in place to nourish your pumpkins.

Once you have chosen your final set fruit, and your plant has reached appreciable length, you then begin to think more about what the fruit needs for development as opposed to what the vines and roots need. This does not mean that you abandon feeding leaves, roots and vines, but rather means that you shift your fertilizer formulation emphasis to feeding the fruit. Joel Holland calls this approach a balance between vine growth and fruit production. You never want to encourage more vine growth at the expense of development of your pumpkin, but in the same instance, you need a big plant to grow a big pumpkin. So, there must be a balance. Changing fertilizer strategies as growth stages change will help to create this balance.

## Phosphorous

Phosphorous and calcium are very important plant nutrients as they relate to root growth, so they should be stressed during the seedling stage and well into the leaf and root growth stage. Pumpkin vines will root below each leaf everywhere the vine touches the ground. Having adequate phosphorous and calcium in the root zone will insure that roots are active and grow quickly. Having more roots will result in bigger, healthier vines and leaves, and potentially bigger pumpkins.

## Potassium

Potassium aids in the development of carbohydrates in the fruit, so during the fruit growth stage (from fruit set to harvest) you should emphasize this nutrient. Potassium also aids in many of the metabolic functions of the plant, and is essential for any plant that grows as fast as an Atlantic Giant Pumpkin.

The shift in feeding strategies can be accomplished by changing the water soluble fertilizer formulation you use. Peters Plantfoods offers many formulations which can be worked into any feeding program that seeks to take advantage of the specific needs of your plant at various stages of its growth; however, water solubles should be used as enhancers of growth, and should never be used without a thorough use of bulk plant food from manure and concentrated organic and chemical fertilizers.

## Watering

Moisture is essential to growth, and when you consider that 80% of a pumpkin's weight is water, it is easy to see why watering is an important ingredient in growing any world-class, giant pumpkin. Water is also responsible for the movement of plant food to the roots and through the plant's water and nutrient delivery system. Without water, plant food becomes almost unavailable and metabolic functions and carbohydrate development suffer severely, if not end altogether.

Water is universally accepted as essential to growth, however there is much discussion as to how much and when it should be applied. Mother Nature tends to make many of the decisions for us, but occasionally we must introduce more water as either essential moisture, or as a growth enhancer.

Milt Barber claims to have grown his 743 pound pumpkin without much attention and very little water; however, growers like Milt sometimes give new growers the impression that water is not that important. In Milt's case, I venture to guess that his soil is very high in organic matter, holds moisture for very long periods of time, and can withstand long periods of drought. Milt was a dairy farmer for over 30 years, and no doubt, spread the manure from his cows on his fields for 30 years. Annual manure incorporation will result in longer moisture retention in soil. The more manure you add to your soil over time, the less you will have to be concerned with water.

The standard recommendation for pumpkins is that they should receive approximately 1" of rainfall a week, or the equivalent by manual means. Slightly more than this will enhance growth, but very much more can be as dangerous as no moisture. This statement does not take into consideration the structure of your soil. If you have sandy loam, you will need more water, and if your soil has large amounts of clay and humus, you will need less. High soil moisture levels, combined with a canopy of leaves shading the soil can create ideal conditions for the spread of diseases like powdery mildew and gummy stem blight. A flood of water can also temporarily deprive your plant's roots of oxygen, much the same as drowning.

The important things to remember about watering is to do it moderately and within guidelines that enhance the growth of your pumpkin plant if at all possible. Water should be applied directly to the soil, and not overhead onto the leaves. This practice will prevent the spread of disease on leaves and stems, and will also prevent the premature removal of insecticides or fungicides that you have applied to the plant. This is only advice. Many of us will not have the luxury of watering in any other fashion but overhead, but precautions should be applied if you are relying on overhead sprinklers as your only source of water.

*Above: Catastrophic stem split can vastly reduce the potential of a giant pumpkin without abruptly ending its growing.*

# *Chapter 12 Insect and Disease Protection*

Controlling both insects and diseases on pumpkins is very important. Most growers learn this the hard way though. Among competitive growers there is the attitude that growing experience is one of the most important elements of their success. This experience includes the failures that they have made along the way in not controlling various insects and diseases.

*Right: Insecticides and fungicides can help to reduce the chances of infestations of many pests, but are not absolutely necessary. Most growers use them only to optimize growth and control any limiting factors of growth.*

There is much truth to this belief, but the use of insect and disease controls can reduce the time it takes to become a competitive grower. By eliminating some of the more troublesome pests, you will have a better chance of growing healthy, vigorous plants and large pumpkins. You could learn how to control insects and diseases by reading this book and other articles on control, and then implement this knowledge. Or you can choose to wait until the damage occurs and vow to eliminate its reoccurrence next year. The second way of responding is what most growers refer to as experience, the first is being smart.

Preventative controls must be in place if you are to successfully combat insects and diseases which are detrimental to the growth of pumpkin plants. You can grow without these controls, but your chances of growing a truly giant pumpkin will be reduced and most pumpkins you grow without controls will never reach their true potential.

## INSECTS

The most devastating of insects to pumpkin plants are few, and you may not encounter some of them in your region of the country. Each region of the US seems to have its "Public Enemy #1" when it comes to insects. In the Northeast it may be Cucumber Beetles, in the Midwest, Vine Borers and in the West, perhaps Squash Bugs. Except for some of the colder pumpkin growing regions, like Southern Canada, most of these pests will appear at one time or another if you grow pumpkins long enough. The few you should be aware of will be among the group we discuss in this chapter. They include: Squash Vine Borers, Squash Bugs, Cucumber Beetles and Aphids.

## Squash Vine Borers

The Squash Vine Borer is common to some parts of Southern Canada and the United States east of the Rocky Mountains. Its prey all seem to be among the Cucumber Family in which squash, gourds, cucumbers, melons and pumpkins belong.

Its life cycle is fairly simple, and a knowledge of it is essential in controlling its numbers. From egg to larvae to pupae to moth, the Squash Borer lives a life in which it is ever changing in appearance. The female adult moth is about the size of a wasp with a greenish brown body, translucent wings, a red to orange striped abdomen and 5 red spots positioned in a row down the length of her back. She moves with darting and flickering movements which are reminiscent of a Dragon Fly. She lays eggs singly on leaf stems and vines. These eggs are oval, flat and brownish The eggs hatch out white larvae with brown heads which quickly bore into vines and begin to feed on the tissue inside. You can usually find evidence of them by looking for frass (excrement) and holes along the vine. This greenish-yellow frass is your first tip that you have an invader. Once you see this, you may not be able to control the borer with insecticides, and may have to perform surgery on the vine to extract the borer. Once inside the vine, the borer is protected from chemical sprays. Plants plagued by vine borers soon wilt and die, while the larvae spin cocoons in which to hibernate as pupae to await the next season.

These over-wintering pupae are normally found in the top 1–5" of soil and they will predictably emerge from the soil as adults between June 8th and the 15th in southern New England. They will emerge up to 3 weeks earlier in the South and somewhat later in the North. The important thing to understand is that their adult life is fairly short, perhaps 6–8 weeks. The emerging female will immediately begin laying eggs on stems and vines, and will continue for about 4–5 weeks. This means that effective control can be obtained if you are diligent during the egg-laying period. In southern New England, thoroughly spraying leaves, stems and vines from about June 10th until July 20th will give good control.

*Above: A closeup shot of the dreaded Squash Vine Borer.*
*Below: The resulting damage of a Squash Vine Borer infestation.*

Most growers use either Sevin or Methoxychlor as the mainstays in their insecticide control programs. It is interesting to note that Sevin is not labeled as a control for Squash Vine Borer, but experience has taught most growers that it is very effective in reducing the egg-laying of adult moths

on leaves and stems, and therefore successful in reducing vine borers. Since both of these insecticides have fairly short residual periods (the time in which they are active deterrents), they must be sprayed periodically and consistently throughout the growing season. A once-a-week spraying should give good control, with additional sprays required when excessive rain or overhead watering has washed chemical residues off of leaves and stems. Sprays should be directed at all of the plant parts, especially the leaf stems which seem to be the likely target of egg laying moths. Spraying should be done after the sun has begun to set in the evening. It is at this time that flower blossoms will begin to close and bees will be less active in the garden. Sevin is very toxic to bees, and any spraying during the day should be refrained from. Spraying after 7–8 PM prevents insecticide from penetrating the interior of blossoms, since they are closed. When these blossoms open the following morning, bees will be free to roam in and out of them without coming in contact with the insecticide.

In place of Sevin or other chemical insecticides, some organic growers will use Rotenone, diatomaceous earth and Bt. They are fairly effective in controlling the larvae stage, but do nothing in hindering the adult in her egg laying activities. Since she lays her eggs singly, the chances of finding all of these single egg locations are very slim. Once the larvae is inside the vine, only extraction can prevent it from totally killing that section of the vine. Extracting the borer can be as injurious to the plant as the borer itself, and much care must be taken to prevent the entrance of diseases into the plant's system after the extraction. It is better to prevent the borer from entering in the first place, and this can only be prevented by deterring the adult moths.

Other non-chemical procedures which will help in reducing borers are fairly simple practices. Since the pupae over-winter in the top 1–5" of soil, frequent cultivation before planting will reduce their numbers later. Begin this in the Fall, and continue right up until planting. Also, burning infected vines will kill any active borers that are contained in them. These practices should be followed by any grower, regardless of using chemical or organic insecticides.

## Squash Bugs

This large beetle, sometimes measuring .75" long, can do enormous damage to all vine crops and especially pumpkin plants. Most commonly called the "Stink Bug" because of its odor when crushed, it lays its brick-red eggs in masses or clusters on leaves. Eggs hatch out tiny nymphs which have greenish brown bodies and reddish heads. Both nymphs and adults are voracious eaters, with plants showing extreme wilt from their presence. This wilting is the result of a toxic substance that the bug injects into the plant, and causes the eventual blackening of leaves. They can be controlled with normally used insecticides, and any program of spraying should be stepped up when egg masses are observed.

## Cucumber Beetles

Striped Cucumber Beetles measure approximately .25" and have black bodies with three yellow stripes running the length of their wings. This tenacious visitor, in numbers, can completely defoliate new seedlings in a

*Below: A Striped Cucumber Beetle is not only a ferocious eater of pumpkin leaves but is also the culprit in the spread of the dreaded disease, Bacterial Wilt.*

single day, and can aid in the spread of diseases and bacterial wilt. The larvae stage lives and over-winters in the soil, so frequent cultivation prior to planting is advised. Also frequent spraying with a general insecticide combined, perhaps, with a covering of floating row material should give you satisfactory control. I have found that floating row material is an essential ingredient in growing giant pumpkins, because it has so many uses. It can keep insects such as vine borers, cucumber beetles and aphids entirely off plants, and at the same time, give limited protection from minor frosts. As an organic control, Rotenone seems to be very effective in reducing the number of adult Cucumber Beetles, so its use is highly advised.

## Aphids

This very small insect, measuring less than a thirty-second of an inch, sucks the sap from leaves, stems and blossoms. What it lacks in size, it more than makes up for in its prodigious reproductive activities. You will rarely ever see just one aphid (they are just too small), rather you will see colonies of hundreds which could easily fit on the tip of your finger.

Many varieties exist, mostly noted by the color of their bodies, which can be yellow, brown, green or black. They are not easily spotted because of their size and color, and overlooking them for only short periods of time will give them ample time to reproduce at very high rates. They also frequently congregate on the underside of leaves where they are less likely to be detected. Their sucking activities can cause leaf curl and leaf puckering. They secrete a sugary substance that is particularly craved by ants. A sure tip that you have aphids in your plants will be the presence of ants. Aphids are more active during hot weather, and their puncturing of leaf surfaces prior to sucking causes these areas to be more susceptible to diseases which are prevalent during the warmer times of Summer.

### DISEASES

The most common diseases effecting pumpkins are Damping-Off, Downy and Powdery Mildew, Gummy Stem Blight, Sclerotinia Stem Rot, Bacterial Wilt and Watermelon Mosaic.

## Damping-Off

When damping-off hits, seedlings either rot in the ground or collapse soon after emerging. Infected seedlings are dull reddish brown lesions are occasionally observed. Seedlings literally rot, resulting in death or severely reduced vitality.

The conditions for damping-off are associated with high moisture levels either from excessive watering, poor soil aeration or lack of adequate ventilation. Any soil compacting which retards or delays the movement of the seedling as it attempts to emerge from the soil will increase the chances of contracting damping off fungus.

Treating seed with a general fungicide such as Captan, and spraying of the soil for several feet around the seedling is highly advised. Good quality, vigorous seed will also reduce the effects of damping-off. Aggressive seed

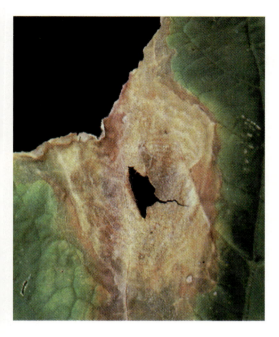

*Above: Gummy Stem blight often starts on leaf margins, then invades the whole plant.*
*Below: The results of a Gummy Stem Blight infestation can hardly be called mild. Severe wilt followed by death of the plant is almost inevitable.*

which quickly germinates and quickly pushes its seed leaves through the soil to sunlight, is the best defense against damping-off. Once into the sunlight and air, seedlings are less prone to excessive moisture and high humidity associated with low ventilation conditions.

It is a common practice to sterilize soil or use sterilized soil media to germinate seeds in prior to transplanting to the growing area. Using sterilized media to start seeds vastly improves the chances of raising good, healthy seedlings without damping-off fungus becoming a problem.

## Gummy Stem Blight

Gummy Stem Blight is common to all vine crops and occurs on all plant parts of them. It can effect seedlings as well as mature plants. Infected stems often develop cankers which secrete a reddish-brown, gummy fluid, hence the name. On fruit, the disease starts as green spots which gradually enlarge turning deep brown in color. These spots may also have gummy secretions associated with them. On leaves, the disease often starts on leaf margins, and then gradually invades the entire leaf, causing severe wilt and death to the leaf.

Gummy Stem Blight is most prevalent during warm weather combined with prolonged rain or high humidity. The fungus over-winters on plant residue, so careful collection of residue plant materials, and burning, are the best ways to reduce chances of the disease.

Since high humidity is ideal for its spread, spraying programs should be stepped-up during these times. Also, overhead watering, which introduces moisture to leaf surfaces, should be avoided if at all possible. General fungicides like Captan and Daconil control this disease very well, and should be used as preventative programs as opposed to programs used to stop the spread of an already existing problem.

## Sclerotinia Stem Rot

All cucurbits are susceptible to this fungus which thrives in high moisture and high humidity when temperatures are cool. Its appearance is marked by a white, cottony growth on the leaves, fruit and particularly susceptible stems. Main and secondary vines can literally disintegrate where infected, leaving only the tough fibrous xylem. Plants quickly and irreversibly turn yellow and die. Sclerotinia is a soil fungus, and because it can live in the soil for many years, normal crop rotation and cultivation methods only slightly reduce its occurrence. This disease is one that should be prevented. It will appear if pumpkin plants are left unprotected. If you do not use a preventative disease control program, you will be inviting this visitor for lunch. The most susceptible times of the growing season are the Fall, when soil moisture levels are high and temperatures begin to decline.

## Bacterial Wilt

Bacterial Wilt is less common than other diseases effecting pumpkins, but can become a problem if you are prone to attacks from Cucumber Beetles. The bacteria cannot survive from one season to the next on infect-

Top: Sclerotinia Stem Rot is characterized by the cottony growth on leaves, fruit and stems.
Bottom: Bacterial Wilt takes its toll on the pumpkin patch, and ends any hopes of a championship pumpkin this year.

ed debris. The bacteria proliferates and spreads by the feeding of Striped and Spotted Cucumber Beetles. The beetles ingest the bacteria while eating the pumpkin's leaves or other host plants, then passes the disease to other leaves as they feed. The best control for Bacterial Wilt is a good insect control program which eliminates, or drastically reduces the population of Cucumber Beetles.

## Watermelon Mosaic

Watermelon Mosaic appears on pumpkins during the very warm, high humidity times of the growing season. It first develops as a yellowing between leaf veins, and gradually deteriorates the entire leaf, leaving only the main leaf veins remaining. The disease is spread mostly by insects such as aphids and mites, and by manual means via gardening tools. There are no disease controls that are effective against it, so your first line of defense should be adequate control of insects which carry the virus, improved sanitation if areas of your garden are infected and thorough removal and burning of infected debris.

## Downy Mildew

The leaves of pumpkins infected by Downy Mildew will display yellow spots which remain restrained in growth between leaf veins. As these infected areas develop, their color turns tan to brown with a white to gray mold appearing on the underside of the infected leaves. A severe infestation will result in leaf loss, reduced plant vitality and poor development of fruit.

*Above: Watermelon Mosaic starts as a yellowing of leaves between veins, and gradually kills the entire leaf. Here it is shown on Zucchini. Below: A closeup of Watermelon Mosaic with its characteristic start confined between leaf veins.*
*Right: The advanced stages of Downy Mildew leaves a pumpkin plant withered and lacking its green lush appearance.*

## Powdery Mildew

Powdery Mildew appears as light yellow spots that eventually become covered by white spores. These spores give the appearance of powder on the leaf. Powdery Mildew can infect both sides of the leaves as well as stems. Infected plants develop yellowing leaves which eventually die. Infection takes place when high humidity conditions are present. The disease is especially active when high densities of leaf growth prevent normal air flow from drying the plant's parts. Night time dew are good conditions for its spread.

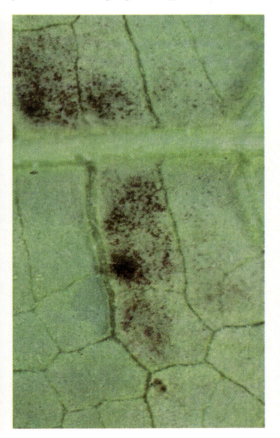

## INSECT AND DISEASE CONTROLS

The control of insects and diseases on pumpkins will be a continuous task throughout the growing season, and may very well extend before and after the season if certain cultural practices are followed. Your spray program will begin with seed planting.

It is advised that some general fungicide be applied to seeds prior to planting. A coating of Captan or Sulfur can reduce damping off fungus and other diseases which cause seed to rot in the ground. You can buy Captan as a dust or wettable powder. Since you will be spraying throughout the

*Above: Powdery mildew with its characteristic white powdery covering, can infect both sides of leaves.*
*Left: This picture shows a plant infected with powdery mildew on the left and a resistant variety on right. Plant breeders are constantly looking for disease and insect resistant varieties .*
*Below: The late stages of powdery mildew reduce a pumpkin plant to a mere shadow of itself.*

growing season, it seems more advantageous to purchase a wettable powder. Captan is generally sold as a 50% wettable. This means that 50% of its weight contains the active ingredient, Captan. Follow the directions on the package closely. It is also suggested that in addition to coating the seed with a general fungicide that you also spray the soil for several feet around the initial planting area. This further reduces the chances of damping off. You should also combine an insecticide with this spraying to control ground insects that could emerge and defoliate your new seedlings. These general insecticides could be: Diazinon, Rotenone, Malathion, Methoxychlor or Sevin.

Most growers use a combination of insecticides to give broader control of insects, and tank mix a fungicide with them throughout the growing season. Captan and Daconil seem to be most widely used with some growers using both while others rotate the use of each at every spraying.

After planting of seeds or seedlings, spraying should occur on a weekly basis. This program should be followed quite rigorously, and stepped-up to twice a week if pests become evident. You should be particularly observant of insects such as aphids, cucumber beetles, squash bugs and adult squash vine borers. When they are present, extra spraying applications may be required. Spraying should also be repeated if heavy rain or prolonged over-head watering washes chemical residues off of leaves, stems, vines and fruit. When spraying, it is important to get thorough coverage of all the plant's parts. If not protected with a preventative spray, each part can become susceptible to some form of insect or disease infestation. It is also advised that a wetting agent, or "spreader/sticker" be included in your tank mixing of insecticides and fungicides. This oil prevents water from rolling off leaf parts, and spreads the mixture thinly and evenly over the plant's surface.

When spraying, wear protective clothing, including long sleeved shirts, gloves and masks to prevent injury to yourself. Although the products mentioned in this chapter are "off-the-shelf" products found at most lawn and garden stores, they should be used with extreme caution and all information on packaging should be read and followed strictly.

Organic insect and disease controls can substitute some of the chemical products. Rotenone does a fair job of controlling general insect infestations, while Bt can control leaf chewing caterpillars if it is present where they are feeding. Since Bt must be ingested, it must be on every inch of the plant's parts to give total control of vine borers. This may be next to impossible. In addition, the use of organic insecticides, which have very short residual periods, means more sprayings and less protection between sprayings.

Sulfur is used as a general, organic fungicide. It can be purchased as either a wettable powder or as a dust. It is a safer fungicide than Captan or Daconil, so it gets a lot of use at the end of the season when more people are likely to be touching your prized pumpkin.

Both Captan and Sulfur are used on plant parts which suffer cracks or tears, or anywhere on the plant where openings in its protective covering occur. Anywhere that the plant suffers cracks or fissures exposes the plant's internal system to disease. Some growers will make a paste from Captan or Sulfur to manually apply to areas suffering stress, particularly around the stem, on the fruit and along the vine.

The important thing to remember about your spray program is that it is easier to control insects and diseases than it is to eradicate them after they get a foothold in your pumpkin patch. Virus infections and Squash Vine Borers may never appear if you spray routinely, but will systematically destroy your crop if they are allowed to get started.

Set up a weekly routine of spraying, and be particularly observant of what pests are active. If certain insects or diseases seem to be escalating, step-up your spray program until they are eliminated. Any good program of control for insects and diseases, as well as weeds and grasses, starts early so that major problems do not materialize.

*Above: A weed free pumpkin patch guarantees an aggressive plant, and an aggressive pumpkin plant guarantees a weed-free garden.*

# Chapter 13 Weed and Grass Control

Controlling weeds and grasses in the garden contains no real glamour. There will never be the excitement we feel when we plant our seeds, pollinate flowers or harvest pumpkins. It is one of the necessary routines all gardeners must be prepared to carry out if they are to grow healthy, vigorous plants. It gets very little attention in writings and discussions about growing plants, but commands most of the grower's time during the growing season.

Keeping weeds and grasses in check during the Summer in an area large enough to grow 1, 2 or more giant pumpkins is a large task, yet controlling weeds and grasses is the very reason why some gardeners are good growers, while others are not. I believe that attention to weed and grass problems is what distinguishes one with a "green thumb" from an ordinary gardener. Eliminating competing plants in your garden means that your intended crop gets full benefit from the soil, moisture and anything you add to the growing area. All the fertilizer, spraying and soil preparation does little if weeds and grasses are allowed to grow at their own rate.

I am a firm believer that chemical controls of weeds and grasses (herbicides) can produce as much harm to the pumpkin plant as it does to the weeds it kills. There is a fine line between controlling weeds and grasses and causing diminished production in your intended crop. Growers frequently cross this line reducing the vitality and potential of their pumpkins. I do not know any top growers who use chemical controls. All use cultural procedures which have been the hallmark of gardening for centuries. Gentle cultivation periodically throughout the growing season is the best form of weed and grass control.

Implements for cultivation can be as simple as a gardening rake or hoe and as sophisticated as a tractor-drawn plow or rototiller. In the end, manual labor will be the primary source of energy. Some growers actually like to cultivate, finding solace and therapeutic comfort from it. Doing some cultivation every day insures that weeds and grasses never get any growth momentum started. The grower who lightly treads through his pumpkin patch with hoe or rake in hand to combat the small newly germinated seeds of weeds and grasses stands the best chance of eliminating huge problems later.

Rototilling and heavier equipment can be used in areas where pumpkin roots have not ventured. It is important to understand that a giant pumpkin's root system is as giant as the plant itself. It goes everywhere that the vines go, and sometimes extends beyond the reach of the vines. Perimeter tilling and plowing is advised to reduce labor in those areas beyond the reach of vines, but within the active root growing area of the plant, long handled tools and hands should be your only implements.

There is the consolation that if weed and grasses are kept under control early, they will not be a problem later. The canopy of cover that the large leaves of a giant pumpkin produces, shades the ground sufficiently so that newly germinated seeds of weeds and grasses never gain the growth momentum they would otherwise have in full sunlight. The key thing to remember in controlling weeds and grasses is to do it early, and do it often.

You may even come to enjoy weeding. Some do. Most that do enjoy it are those that perform the necessary cultivation requirements when they are needed, and do not postpone them. Weeding only becomes a chore and headache when it is left undone for a few weeks. It is much easier and less arduous if cultivation is done every 2–3 days.

This day-to-day cultivation will also put you in closer contact with your plants. You will be benefiting from closer observations of developments which may require action before they escalate. While weeding, you may come across insect damage, varmint damage or the beginnings of a disease infestation. Hand cultivating every 2-3 days will guarantee that any problem will not go undiscovered for very long.

## Mulches

Some growers use mulches to reduce the chances that weed and grasses will start in the first place. Some use grass clippings, rotted manure, and where available, compost. Others use no mulches, relying on the living mulch of huge pumpkin leaves to do the job. Some growers have even experimented with black plastics and other weed-blocking fabrics, but none, to my knowledge has had great success. The pumpkin's vines will root everywhere that a leaf is present. If soil is not available below a leaf axil, then roots are thwarted in their efforts. Some use plastic on the entire growing area, and remove it gradually as the plant advances. This appears to require the same amount of effort as hand cultivating, but is much more costly. Perimeter plowing and tilling can accomplish the same thing at no cost to the grower.

## Summary

Control of weeds and grasses should begin early and continue often throughout the growing season. Eliminating weeds before they accelerate in growth is your best line of defense against them.

# Chapter Fourteen Varmint Control

There are not many things that are more discouraging to gardeners than the loss of plants due to varmints. Anyone who has had a vegetable garden mowed-down by woodchucks knows the feeling. Overnight, small, prized, seedlings can be chomped to the ground with only a small bit of the stem protruding to mark their existence. The frustration mounts when a grower begins to feel helpless after many unsuccessful attempts are made to protect his plants. This frustration may lead to rage, and anyone who has ever seen the movie *Caddy Shack* knows that frustration and rage can lead to some very bizarre behavior when it comes to efforts aimed at eliminating varmints.

The most common critters to be cautious of are woodchucks, field mice, moles and rabbits. Each has its own strategy of destruction. Field mice will live in nearby refuse or under heavy mulch in the garden. At night they will emerge to nibble the fruit of your pumpkins. A night's work can lead to the elimination of a pumpkin from the category of prize specimen. In addition, this gnawing will allow disease to more easily get started, and can lead to premature rotting of the fruit.

Moles will do much the same thing, but are more secretive in their attempts. A mole can burrow beneath your pumpkin, and then emerge below it to feast undetected. Many times the mole is only discovered at harvest when a gaping hole is revealed as the pumpkin is rolled from the garden.

Rabbits are less destructive, concentrating their feeding on leaves (which are large and many). The feeding of one rabbit presents no problem, but a band of visitors, making repeated trips for dinner, can be quite discouraging.

The methods of eliminating or reducing damage caused by these varmints pales in comparison to what growers will do to eliminate their arch rival, the woodchuck. Field mice can be prevented, eliminated or controlled by the placing of rodenticide baits near the pumpkin patch. Traps and devices used to catch and spear mice and moles are also sold. These devices seem more destructive, but produce the same results as rodenticide poisoning. Keeping mulches well worked will also disturb them, and with repeated efforts, they may abandon their claim to your pumpkin. In large garden areas with many plants and pumpkins to protect, this may be a difficult task. Being observant of mice and mole activity can also help you to thwart their efforts at destroying your giant pumpkin. Mole tunnels, which are small arched runways protruding from the surface of the soil, are easy to spot. If one of these tunnels leads to a pumpkin, you had best start to excavate the area to flush the visitor from his home. Rabbits can be controlled with fences or by luring them to companion plantings of leafy vegetables such as lettuce, Swiss chard or beets. They will choose the tender leaves of these plants before eating the prickly leaves of your pumpkin.

## Woodchucks

No critter confounds growers more than the woodchuck. This varmint, known by many other names regionally, is smart, alert and never ventures far from the protection of its underground den. Whatever name you call them: woodchuck, groundhog, whistle pig or gopher, your energy and skill will be tested in the battle to keep them from your pumpkin patch. These critters can weigh up to 10 pounds and measure 20 inches long. They have curved claws on their front feet which makes them amazingly adept diggers. Anyone who has a family of woodchucks living nearby knows the damage they create in the landscape. In one Summer, they can change level ground into a field of moguls. The soil from the underground den is deposited above the main entrance. At least one other exit exists, and it could be up to 60 feet away, although it is most commonly found within 10-15 feet of the main entrance. This den is an ingenious form of housing. The entrance and exit holes produce an effective ventilation of air, while the deep burrow is protected from the hot weather of Summer and the freezing ground of Winter. Woodchucks hibernate in these dens from about November to March. They spend the better part of the growing season feeding a voracious appetite aimed at increasing their body fat so they can withstand 4–5 months of hibernation.

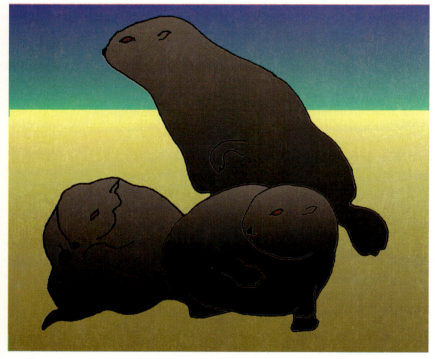

Females mate in early-Spring producing litters which range from 2–4 offspring. These young chucks will be completely weaned by mid-Summer, and on their own to feed and find homes. They will generally move into abandoned dens while their parents constantly prepare new ones closer to feeding sites.

They are daylight feeders, but generally confine their feeding to early morning (just after dawn) and evening (just before sunset). You will rarely see them mid-day, except in late season when feeding becomes frantic before the hibernation period begins.

There are many strategies used for protecting pumpkins from them. Wire fencing, buried several inches in the ground can be a deterrent. Some growers have used electric fences like those commonly used to control cows and horses. Others prefer to use rifles with telescopic sights. These telescopic sights are essential because you may never meet a woodchuck up close with a rifle in your hand. Their hearing and eyesight are very acute, and anything out of the ordinary will see them bolting to the safety of a nearby den. You will occasionally get good sights on a woodchuck, but you had better hit him the first time. There will be no second opportunity.

Gas cartridges may be purchased at a local garden center. These cartridges are ignited then placed inside the burrow. All exits are then blocked with soil so that the gases are prevented from escaping. Carbon monoxide fills the den and the unsuspecting woodchuck dies from suffocation. This method can be effective if you have only one or a few dens, but if you have several generations nearby, the amount of burrows will be staggering. And, since many of these dens will be vacant, it becomes a "crap shoot" as to what burrow to pick for gassing.

Trapping seems to create the best results with woodchucks. The use of live traps like the Havahart Trap™, baited with leafy vegetables, melon or apples can be very effective. In this way, captured woodchucks can be handled in a more humane way. However, check the laws of your state or region, because live trapping with the intent of transporting to other areas may be illegal.

# Chapter 15 Pollination and Fruit Setting

*Above: Hand pollinating a female flower with a specially prepared male flower is easily done and helps control genetic characteristics.*

Pumpkins have the ability to root wherever they touch the soil. Anchor roots develop beneath almost every leaf. This is the pumpkin's way of securing itself to the ground and a method of gathering more plant nutrients. This is also why we prepare all the soil in the garden area and not just in the hill containing the young plant. Your pumpkin will feed from every square foot of garden area that it covers.

During this stage of growth, pollination of the plant also occurs. Pollination is the act of delivering pollen from the male flowers to the female flower parts. Pumpkins contain both male and female flowers on the same plant. Pollination is most often accomplished by bees, but serious pumpkin growers seek to control the process. By selectively pollinating female flower parts with specific male pollen, then protecting the female flower from any outside intervention, the grower seeks to improve the characteristics of the resulting seed. Selective hand-pollination also gives the grower more control, even if he is not concerned with the characteristics of the resulting seed. He can control where the pumpkin will be on the plant.

You may pollinate female flowers with pollen from any male pumpkin flower either on the plant or on another pumpkin plant. The act of pollinating a female flower with pollen from a male flower on another plant is called cross-pollination. In this case, the characteristics of the newly introduced male will effect the genes of the seed that results from pollination. Your pumpkin will always be the result of a pollinated female flower; therefore, all pumpkins are female in gender. Don't forget this if you decide to name your pumpkin as growers often do.

Fruit set, which is the sign of a successful pollination, should occur when the vine is big enough and the weather conditions are optimal for growth. Some growers wait until fruit set occurs naturally before beginning hand-pollination. Later they cull the naturally pollinated fruit if it does not measure up to other candidates on the vine. Others believe that vine length and leaf counts should be at certain minimums before pollination occurs. Most giant pumpkins are grown several feet from the initial planting site on vines which are already 10–15' long. It is believed that to grow a truly giant pumpkin it must be positioned on a vine at least 10' long. Waiting until these requirements exist means that your fruit will be set on a large plant already in place to fuel the growth of the pumpkin. A new theory suggests that the first set-fruit will be the largest regardless of its position on the vine. Growers have grown large pumpkins closer to the hill, on shorter vines, but most will agree that further out on the vine gives higher probability of giant weights. It is also recommended that the pumpkin be set on the main vine as opposed to secondary vines (side shoots) which might exist.

Wayne Hackney, a very successful New England pumpkin grower says he has,

> *"Never had a pumpkin over 410 pounds that was set within 6 feet from the base of the plant."*

However, Ray Waterman grew his 780.5-pounder only 6' out.

Fruit set should occur about mid-July. This is a compromise between adequate growth of the plant already established, and length of the season remaining for development of the pumpkin. If you pollinate much before July 1st, you will be doing it on shorter vines (smaller plants). If you wait much later than mid-July, you may not have enough time remaining in the growing season to develop a really giant pumpkin. Obviously, these dates are from my experience as a New England grower growing on the 42nd latitude. Your region of the country may have dates which begin earlier than those listed above. Ask veteran growers in your area, or write to any of the *Heavy Hitters* who live near you.

It is important to pollinate many female flowers at the same time. The rate of pollination failure is very high in pumpkins. Temperature, stress and incomplete pollination can all abort the new fruit. You must take this into consideration. Try to set 3–4 pumpkins, and then only after 2–3 weeks of growth begin culling the less vigorous. This insures that you will have at least one pumpkin set on your plant. Fortunately, bees do a very good job at completely pollinating pumpkins without grower help.

Some growers count leaves, and refrain from pollinating until a certain number are present on the plant. This is logical in that leaves are like solar panels collecting the sun's energy. The more leaves you have, the more of the sun's energy can be used. I have heard recommendations that 200–500 leaves should exist on the plant before hand-pollination begins. Again, less leaves means shorter vines and less plant to support the new pumpkin, while more leaves means longer vines, but less season remaining for development of the fruit. Hand-pollinating is always a compromise between plant size and the remaining days of the season.

Other growers let Mother Nature alone handle the pollination of female flowers and fruit set, while still others embrace hand-pollinating, but also allow pollination by bees to help insure complete pollination. Unprotected female flowers, pollinated by bees, may be crosses with other pumpkins in the garden or in the vicinity, and can never be totally reliable in terms of seed offspring characteristics. This is fine since not all growers want to, or need to, know the parents of their pumpkin's seed. This information is nice to know, especially if you grow an extraordinarily large pumpkin, but if pumpkin growing is just a way to have fun for you, then controlling pollination is not really necessary.

## How Do You Hand-Pollinate

Hand pollination begins with establishing the right time, the right plant size and the right growing conditions to optimize pumpkin development. All hand-pollination should take place when plants (vines) are large

*Above: Howard Dill waters a pumpkin plant at the ideal size for fruit setting. Runners are 10-12' long. Notice also how well weeds are controlled in the patch.*

enough. Good locations for that monster pumpkin will be anywhere from 10–15' out on the vine. You will have many opportunities to selectively hand-pollinate or cross-pollinate within 4–6 weeks of initial planting. Hand-pollinating should be done very early in the morning, as soon after sunrise as possible on newly-opened flowers.

Hand-pollinating requires some advance planning and a commitment to carry out these plans. Freshly opened male and female flowers are your best candidates. Selecting likely candidates the day before they open will become second nature to you after a few weeks of observation, and is highly advised. Look for flowers that are just ready to open. The evening before is a good time to look for your potential candidates. Mark them by covering them with cheesecloth, paper bags or something similar. Covering them will not only mark their location, but also protect them from any bees that might beat you to them the next day. Bees will be up very early in search of nectar, which is present in both the female and male flowers. The act of moving from flower to flower by bees never fails to distribute pollen from the male flowers to the female. Some growers will mark their candidates by other means and leave the flowers unprotected from bees with the belief that bees will do a better job of pollinating than man could ever accomplish. Hand-pollination should occur very early in the morning on freshly opened flowers. These fresh flowers are the ripest for successful pollination.

*Left: A female flower is characterized by its multi-segment stigma located in the interior of the flower. Each stigma contains a passageway to a separate ovary within the fruit attached to the flower's base.*

Each female flower is made up of flower parts that differentiate it from male flowers. Male flowers are quite upright, suspended on thin stems while female flowers have thicker, shorter stems and possess a small pumpkin at the base of their blossoms. Inside the male blossom there are many thin filaments topped by plant parts called anthers which form the pollen. This entire plant part is referred to as the stamen. Pumpkin pollen grains are very large, and unlike pollen from many other plants, can be seen with the naked eye. Inside the female flower you will find a flower part referred to as the pistol. Each pistol is made up of a stigma, a style and an ovary. The stigma is the receptacle for the pollen, while the style is the thin passageway leading

Right: A male flower is characterized by its single stamen. This stamen produces the pollen from which female flowers are pollinated.

from the stigma to the ovary located within the small pumpkin attached to the base of the blossom. Female pumpkin blossoms are characterized by having multiple stigma, styles and ovaries. Growers refer to these as segments, but they are also referred to as stigmas, carpels or lobes. Each segment is clearly visible when the blossom opens. Most pumpkins have 3–4 segments, meaning that they have 3 or 4 separate ovaries within the pumpkin. Each ovary, if properly fertilized will produce its own pocket of seeds within the pumpkin. The number of segments will vary from flower to flower with 5-segment flowers occurring quite often and 6 and 7-segment flowers appearing on occasion. Although it has not been scientifically proven, 5-segment flowers seem to bear larger pumpkins than 3 or 4-segment flowers. It has not been observed that more than 5 segments will produce larger pumpkins, although the logic of a greater number of seed pockets within the pumpkin seems to suggest the possibility of a heavier pumpkin. 3–4 segment flowers seem to produce lighter pumpkins, although this has never been absolutely proven. The advice from top growers would be to pollinate only blossoms containing at least 5 segments. Choosing several candidates the night before pollinating will give you a better chance of finding a 5-segment flower the next morning.

If seed production is an important characteristic of a giant pumpkin, and many growers think this is so, then the chance for more seed comes from having more seed pockets within the pumpkin. You cannot have 5 seed pockets if you start with a 3-segment flower, so keep this in mind not only when you pollinate, but also when you make your final decision as to what set fruit will remain on the vine and which will be removed.

The physical act of hand-pollinating pumpkins is quite easy to grasp. You merely rub the pollen from the male flower onto the top of the female blossom segments. First, cut the stems of the male blossoms so that they can be moved, then strip the outer flower petals exposing the pistols and pollen. Holding the stem of the male flower, rub the pollen onto the female segments. Some choose to use several male flowers to pollinate one female hoping to better pollinate all the segments. It is not uncommon for incomplete pollination to occur. You could have a 5 segment flower which only matures 3 pockets of seeds. This is the result of incomplete pollination and fertilization. Providing lots of pollen to the flower segments is the only safeguard against incomplete pollination. This is also the reason why some growers leave the female flower exposed to bees after hand-pollination. They hope that bees will do a more complete job of the pollination process. It is interesting to note that each seed pocket within a maturing pumpkin has the chance of producing offspring from different male parents if isolation and protection of the female blossom after pollination is not practiced. Each segment could be pollinated by different male flowers from different pumpkin plants. We cannot control pollination by any means other than isolation and protection after selective hand pollination. If you choose to let Mother Nature take a part in pollination, then each seed pocket within your giant pumpkin may have a different male parent. The seed produced from these different sets of parents will produce seed offspring with uniquely different genes and plant characteristics.

Pollination can be left entirely to the bees. Growers have had good success with this practice, and if time does not permit you to hand-pollinate, then you can still grow a giant pumpkin, but luck will have to be with you if you choose to plant the seeds from this pumpkin the following year.

Selective hand-pollination allows you to track information which will be very helpful to you in future seasons If you grow a really giant pumpkin, you will want to plant the seed from this pumpkin. If you did not control the pollination process, you have no assurance that seed offspring can repeat your achievement. Only by knowing the parents of your giant pumpkin, and selectively hand-pollinating good plant characteristics, can you hope to improve your chances of a similar achievement from your own home-grown seed in future years.

## Choosing the Right Female Flowers

We have already discussed what constitutes a good female candidate. It is one that contains at least 5 flower segments, but their are other considerations which are important in the selection process. How far out on the vine is also quite important and what vine can also be important. An ideal candidate will be on the main vine and between 10–15' from the initial planting place. The juxtaposition of the flower on the vine can also have some bearing on the selection process. A good female candidate should have a stem angle which is almost perpendicular to the vine. If an acute angle exists, the stem will be more likely to be damaged as the pumpkin enlarges. Small angled stems can be modified slowly, but it is better to start with wider stemmed candidates to begin with. We will discuss stem stress more thoroughly in Chapter 17, Pumpkin Protection.

During the leaf and root growth stage, the major priorities to address should be pollination, fruit set, an increased awareness of the plant nutrients responsible for leaf and root growth, and increased provisions for protection of the plant as it relates to insects, disease and weed and grass control. You will learn more on these subjects in Chapters 11, 12 and 13, Fertilizing and Watering, Insect and Disease Control and Weed and Grass Control.

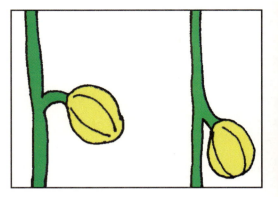

*Above: The fruit on the left has a wider angle which will accommodate the rapid growth of the Dill's Atlantic Giant more easily. Acute angles like those on the right should be avoided.*

# Chapter 16 Pinching and Pruning

P inching and pruning involve the removal of plant parts, like unpollinated fruit and the tips of main, secondary and tertiary vines. Pinching actions are taken in order to divert more of the plant's energy to development of your chosen pumpkins. Pruning, on the other hand, is more radical and is not confined to the tips of vines or small plant parts. When pruning, whole sections of a plant may be removed for the benefit of the plant. Pruning limits sprawl and is used to remove damaged or diseased sections of the plant.

Pinching, or removal of fruit when still small, is a universally accepted practice carried out by all competitive pumpkin growers. Limiting the number of pumpkins on the plant must occur if a giant pumpkin is to be grown. The number of pumpkins you leave on the vine is a subject of some controversy, because there are many top growers who grow 2–4 giants on a single plant, while others limit this number to one pumpkin. There are advantages and disadvantages with either approach, and there are successful growers practicing both methods while producing very large pumpkins.

*Right: Multiple fruit on a vine is the hallmark of all pumpkin plants. Here, the proximity to each other would require the culling of one or the other.*

## Multiple Fruit

The advantages of leaving multiple fruit on the vine are embodied in the old saying that there is protection in numbers. Having more than one fruit on a plant allows for natural disasters which every competitive pumpkin grower will face. Premature ripening, blow-out, cracking and rotting, stem breaks, diseases and damage from insects and varmints can all reduce a pumpkin's chances of obtaining its true potential.

The fact that the size of a giant pumpkin plant dictates that many growers will only be able to grow 1 or 2, means that these few plants must be maximized to their fullest in respects to fruit development. By leaving 3–4 pumpkins on a plant (all on separate vines), a grower is given better chances of having a specimen pumpkin when it is time to harvest and bring it to a weigh-off site at the end of the season. Many giant pumpkins have been grown with equally large companions grown on other vines of the same plant. The key to growing multiple fruit is to have each chosen pumpkin residing on separate, adequately large vines in locations at least 10 feet out on the vine.

A grower always has the option of culling pumpkins from these vines in mid season if they are not sizing up well, or they have developed problems that will keep them from reaching their true potential.

If you are limited by space in the amount of plants you can grow, or your growing conditions present a lot of opportunities for disaster to strike, then multiple fruit seems to be a prudent practice to follow in order to insure that you have something to show for your work at the end of the season.

Don Fleming of Morrisville, Vermont, has long preached the multiple fruit philosophy. Don was the 1985 New England Champ and the 1986 World Champ. With frosts occurring occasionally in July and very cool summertime temperatures, the safety in growing more than one pumpkin on a plant has paid off for him.

Nancy and Peter Rigoloso of Bremerton, Washington, stress leaf count as the determining factor in deciding how many fruit to leave on the plant. Their method allows one pumpkin if the leaf count is less than 800 leaves, two pumpkins if leaf count is between 800 and 1200 and 3 pumpkins if leaves exceed 1200.

Both Joel Holland and Howard Dill evaluate the size and condition of the vine before deciding on additional fruit on the plant. If the vine is well developed, rapidly growing and free from any damage, it becomes a likely candidate for carrying a fruit.

*Above: A single fruit set on a vine almost 20' from the initial planting spot insures a large plant to supply the needs of a large pumpkin.*

## Single Fruit

The single fruit method is practiced by the lion's share of competitive growers. The philosophy of allowing only one pumpkin to benefit from the entire plant is practiced by many world champions and past record holders. The logic is simple to understand. A plant has just so much energy, and its ability to deliver water and nutrients is not infinite. A pumpkin plant is limited in what it can deliver to the fruit set on it. The more fruit on the plant, the smaller the resulting weights of the fruit.

Many growers who practice multiple fruit growth challenge the single fruit stance with data which suggests that more than one large pumpkin can be grown on the same plant, but, world record pumpkins generally come from single fruited plants. The disadvantage of single fruit growth lies in the old saying, "Don't put all your eggs in one basket." If you are a gambler, or have adequate room to grow many plants, then try growing single fruit plants.

Pinching back tertiary vines while still small can eliminate the sprawl produced from the rampant growth of your pumpkin plant. Managing the growth and position of vines will also help to produce the highly sought balance between vine and fruit growth. By limiting vine growth by selective pinching and pruning, fruit growth can be enhanced. As we discussed earlier, some growers count leaves while others measure vine lengths. If you have a long and healthy main and secondary vine with a good pumpkin already growing on it, it will benefit the pumpkin to pinch back tertiary vines along it. You will be helping to balance the scales between vine and fruit growth. Left unpinched, a pumpkin plant will continue to grow vines and new leaves until frost. Many times this growth is at the expense of fruit development. In an *Old Farmer's Almanac* article on *"How to Grow a 1000 Pound Pumpkin"*, the author says of Howard Dill,

> *"After the primary vine has reached 20 feet, he pinches off the tips and the side shoots so the vine won't divert resources from the fruit. He breaks off all the other female flowers."*

Pinching and pruning are practices which all competitive pumpkin growers must follow. Limiting vine growth and culling unwanted pumpkins are some of the ways that a grower can help to determine the destiny of his pumpkin. If you wish to grow truly giant pumpkins, you will have to pinch and prune your plants.

*Below: Margot Skelhorn, the young niece of Howard Dill, toys with an Atlantic Giant Pumpkin from which seed produced Norman Gallagher's 1984-612-pound World Record Pumpkin. This world record earned Norm $10,000 and a trip to Hawaii.*

# Chapter 17 *Pumpkin Protection*

Pumpkin protection differs from an earlier discussion of plant protection in that the practices covered here are geared to protecting the fruit from its own aggressive growth. Plant protection focuses more on the forces of Nature like wind and frost, while pumpkin protection attempts to relieve the stress associated with the natural growth pattern of an Atlantic Giant Pumpkin.

The Atlantic Giant can gain up to 25 pounds a day during the peak of its growing season. This rapid growth presents us with many challenges. Some of these challenges can be met while others have a way of thwarting even the most experienced growers. The unbelievable growth of the fruit can be compared to the filling of a balloon. The skin of the pumpkin stretches, cracks and heals in a drama which at any moment could lead to a gaping crevice, and an end to any further increases in the size of the fruit. Even the smallest of these cracks can allow disease to enter the pumpkin and start a process of rotting which cannot be reversed. As a grower of Atlantic Giant pumpkins you will feel powerless in combat against some of these growth problems. You cannot slow the fruit's development in any appreciable way, and most of us would not want this anyway. Being aware of any cracks and small fissures in the skin of the pumpkin and attending to them immediately seems to be the better course of action. Occasionally, the fruit will grow so fast that it literally blows up, bursting from the shear forces of growth. Growers with very rich soil or programs stressing high fertility seem to experience this phenomena the most; however, this may be a genetic characteristic of the Atlantic Giant. No one has proven either. Many growers combat blowout by going back to "slow and easy" methods of growing pumpkins. They do the same things, but moderate their use.

*Right: A perfect pumpkin specimen, Howard Dill's 493.5-pounder combined thought, preparation and protection.*
*Left Page: A female flower is about to open as the beginning of this year's giant pumpkin is poised at the base.*

Addressing skin cracks will be pretty routine from one Atlantic Giant to another. They are bound to happen, and most of them will quickly heal on their own, but, some could present problems, so it is better to treat all that occur. Competitive growers are keenly aware of skin cracks, and as such, liberally apply fungicides to the fruit in an attempt to protect the pumpkin from contracting diseases. In their once-a-week sprayings of insecticides and fungicides, they make sure that the entire pumpkin is adequately covered with the spray solution. Any cracks that begin to open are quickly mortared with a paste made from a fungicide like Captan. This procedure is followed until the crack heals and hardens. Making and applying poultices from fungicides can come in handy wherever the plant is experiencing damage. Besides the fruit, they are also frequently used on the fruit stem and the vine.

Some growers also place a ground protective covering under their pumpkins while it is still small. This covering helps to protect the fruit from insect or varmint invaders, and may reduce the level of moisture in direct contact with the fruit as well.

Of course, you should not neglect the health of the rest of your pumpkin plant while you are focusing your attention on the fruit. Just because your priority is fruit protection, does not mean you can neglect protecting the entire plant. You cannot grow a large, healthy pumpkin on ailing vines.

## Stem Stress

The stress exerted by the rapidly growing pumpkin on the stem is enormous. The stem does not elongate significantly during the course of the season. It thickens but does not get much longer; however, the growth of the fruit itself is unbelievable. The juncture at which the stem and fruit attach gradually rises in the course of the season. This rising, combined with the fixed length of the stem, provides real force on the stem. The reason why this force is exerted is because the stress resulting from the rising stem connection to the fruit cannot be relieved by the movement of the vines. Vines are solidly rooted to the ground. The vine is anchored to the ground by anchor roots on either side of the fruit. As the pumpkin moves with its natural growth, the vine is fixed to the ground, and all the stress of these opposing forces is exerted on the stem. The stem can literally break loose from the vine, or less dramatically, develop cracks and small tears which leads to its premature rotting and an end to the fruit's huge daily weight gains.

*Above: Gary Keyzer attempts to provide optimum growing conditions for his giant pumpkins. Here he soothes them with a supply of music. No research has validated the success of Gary's method however. Below: Severing the roots for a few feet in either direction of the pumpkin on the vine will allow the vine to rise as the pumpkin's connection to the stem rises.*

Growers will try to relieve this stress by severing the anchor roots on either side of the fruit for 2–3 feet. In this way, as the stem connection to the fruit gradually rises, the vine can also rise as well, relieving the stress on the stem.

## Shoulder/Stem Stress

Another form of stem stress is caused not from the upward movement of stem/fruit juncture, but from the increasing size of the shoulders of the fruit. As the fruit shoulders grow, they push forward. This movement may push the vines away from the fruit causing great pressure on the stem which cannot stretch to accommodate this movement. Even severed anchor

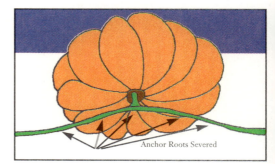

Anchor Roots Severed

*Above: Sy and Cindy Chaponis of Manchester, CT use a bed sheet to provide shade and cooling for one of their prized specimens. Below: Don Fleming and friend examine a large pumpkin beneath a lightweight shade structure.*

roots will not relieve this stress if the shoulders actually grow over and upon the vine. Once on top of the vine, the weight of the pumpkin prevents the movement of the vine and the upward growth of the fruit exerts still greater forces on the stem.

Combating these problems start with the initial fruit selection. Try to pick fruit which are positioned in a wide angle to the stem. Perpendicular to the stem is ideal, while acute angled fruit should not be considered. Each fruit can be moved to a more desirable angle to the vine, but this is a procedure which must be done slowly over a 2–3 week period, and there are no guarantees that you do not do permanent damage to the fruit in the process.

In addition to selecting good, wide angled fruit stems, you can also train vines away from the fruit, so shoulder growth become less of a problem. Training vines away from the fruit gives shoulders more room for growth, and lessens the chance that the fruit will actually touch the vine. Having your pumpkins on the outside of the outermost curve of the vine is ideal. Training vines in this manner is quite easy with stakes, and the direction of the vine can be reversed back to a straighter angle from the fruit once several feet of new vine growth has occurred.

## Shade and Cooling

Hot, direct sun can actually scorch the outer skin of the pumpkin. Direct sunlight causes the pumpkin to toughen its skin making it more brittle and more susceptible to cracking as the fruit enlarges. Top growers provide some form of shade for their prized fruits. These make-shift structures can be quickly created from materials around the house. Some use bed sheets fastened to poles, while others use rain retardant materials attached to moveable frames. Whatever you use, remember to provide ample air ventilation. You are just trying to block the sun, not create greenhouse-like conditions which elevate temperatures. If you shade your pumpkin, its skin will be more supple and better able to expand and stretch as the fruit develops.

Also, many growers apply spray solutions of diluted bleach to the skin of the pumpkin every week to insure that bacteria does not begin to develop. Bleach is a common ingredient used by growers to disinfect pruning tools and other implements in an effort to guard against the spread of diseases from one area to another.

## Summary

Most of the protective measures used by growers are directed at relieving stem stress, or reducing the chance that diseases will be introduced into the fruit prematurely through cracks and fissures in the skin. Selecting a well positioned fruit and directing vines away from it at an early age is critical. Severing roots in either direction around the fruit for 2-3 feet will give the vine freedom to move, thus relieving stress on the stem. Thoroughly spraying the fruit with a general fungicide weekly, and applying poultices made from these fungicides to cracks and crevices will help to prolong the rapid growth of your pumpkin.

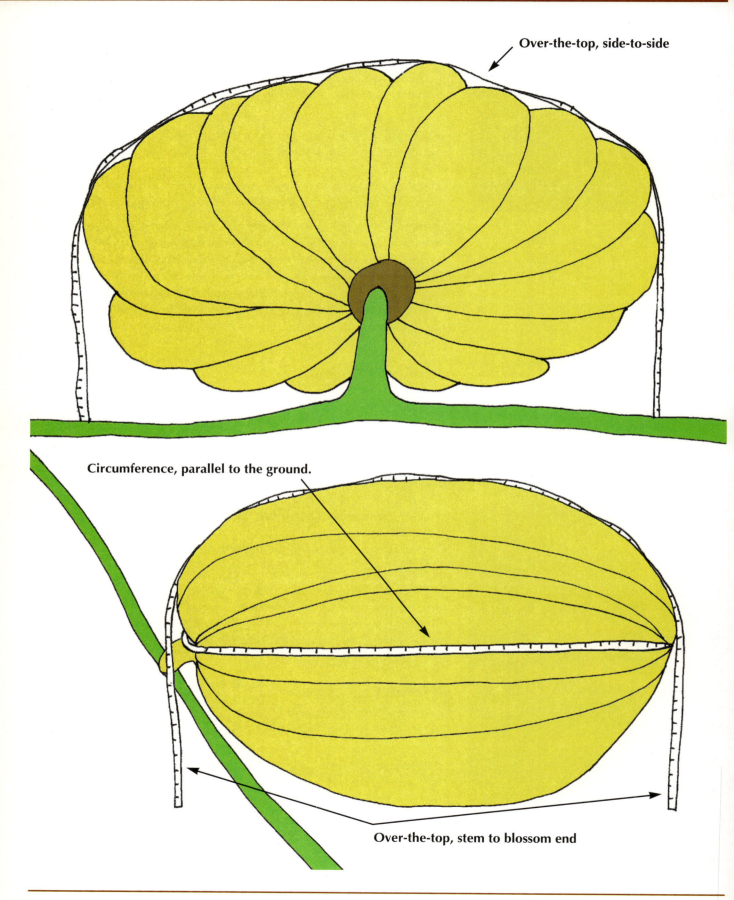

Over-the-top, side-to-side

Circumference, parallel to the ground.

Over-the-top, stem to blossom end

## Chapter 18 *Measuring for Approximate Weight*

### Stellpflug Estimating Method

| Inches | Weight | Inches | Weight | Inches | Weight | Inches | Weight |
|---|---|---|---|---|---|---|---|
| 70 | 93 | 95 | 203 | 120 | 388 | 145 | 669 |
| 71 | 96 | 96 | 208 | 121 | 397 | 146 | 683 |
| 72 | 99 | 97 | 214 | 122 | 407 | 147 | 697 |
| 73 | 103 | 98 | 220 | 123 | 416 | 148 | 711 |
| 74 | 106 | 99 | 227 | 124 | 426 | 149 | 725 |
| 75 | 110 | 100 | 233 | 125 | 436 | 150 | 739 |
| 76 | 113 | 101 | 239 | 126 | 446 | 151 | 753 |
| 77 | 117 | 102 | 246 | 127 | 456 | 152 | 768 |
| 78 | 121 | 103 | 253 | 128 | 467 | 153 | 783 |
| 79 | 125 | 104 | 260 | 129 | 477 | 154 | 798 |
| 80 | 129 | 105 | 267 | 130 | 488 | 155 | 813 |
| 81 | 133 | 106 | 264 | 131 | 499 | 156 | 829 |
| 82 | 137 | 107 | 281 | 132 | 510 | 157 | 844 |
| 83 | 142 | 108 | 288 | 133 | 521 | 158 | 860 |
| 84 | 146 | 109 | 295 | 134 | 532 | 159 | 876 |
| 85 | 151 | 110 | 303 | 135 | 544 | 160 | 892 |
| 86 | 155 | 111 | 311 | 136 | 556 | 161 | 909 |
| 87 | 160 | 112 | 319 | 137 | 568 | 162 | 926 |
| 88 | 165 | 113 | 327 | 138 | 580 | 163 | 943 |
| 89 | 170 | 114 | 336 | 139 | 592 | 164 | 960 |
| 90 | 175 | 115 | 344 | 140 | 604 | 165 | 977 |
| 91 | 180 | 116 | 352 | 141 | 617 | 166 | 994 |
| 92 | 186 | 117 | 361 | 142 | 630 | 167 | 1012 |
| 93 | 191 | 118 | 370 | 143 | 643 | 168 | 1030 |
| 94 | 197 | 119 | 379 | 144 | 656 | 169 | 1048 |

*Above: This table shows inch and weight estimates for giant pumpkins ranging in circumference from 70-169". Reprinted with permission from the WPC.*

Both Howard Dill and Leonard Stellpflug are credited with developing measuring systems for the estimation of weight for large pumpkins and squash. These measurement systems are used by most of the competitive pumpkin growers today. These estimates allow growers to track weight gains on a daily basis, as well as providing a framework within which all growers can compare their pumpkins prior to an official weigh-off. Both systems have appeared in WPC publications. Len Stellpflug's theory first appeared in the *WPC Newsletter* in September 1989, and Howard Dill's "Over-the-Top Method" debuted in the *WPC News Journal* in June 1991.

### Leonard Stellpflug's Method

Stellpflug's method clearly addresses variables like fruit diameter and density, and gives allowances for wall thickness and seed cavity weights. Although this method is an estimate of weight, it has been shown to be quite reliable by growers from all over the US and Canada. Len's equation (Weight = .000213 x Circumference$^3$ + 20) may be a little difficult to understand, but the table constructed for determining weight from circumference measurements is not. The table is presented here with permission from the WPC who holds the copyright on both of these measurement systems.

Without a measurement system, estimating a pumpkin's weight becomes mere guesswork, and comparisons become rooted in non-scientific judgments. With a measurement system, growers have an opportunity to compare their pumpkins with other growers before an actual weight is determined.

In the Stellpflug method, measurements of the circumference of the fruit are taken parallel to the ground at approximately stem height. This measurement will generally provide you with the largest circumference measurement. This measurement is then compared with the Table to provide an estimate of the fruit's weight.

### Howard Dill's Method

Howard Dill's Over-the-Top method of estimating giant pumpkin weights is another reliable method for growers to use. In Dill's method, 3 measurements are added together to determine an estimate of weight. The first measurement is an over-the-top measurement from ground to ground along the axis from stem to blossom end. The second is an over-the-top measurement which is made perpendicular to the stem-blossom-end axis. It is important that these measurement be taken in the correct manner. When measuring over-the-top, the measurement should begin at ground level below the widest portion of the pumpkin. This measurement should not be

*Left Page: Notice that the tape hangs straight down from the sides of the pumpkin in both over-the-top measurements.*

taken at the point in which the pumpkin and ground meet. Hugging the sides of the pumpkin will give an inaccurate estimate of weight. Your tape measure should hang straight down to the ground from the widest point of the pumpkin. The illustration on page 108 will help you to grasp the correct measuring technique. The third measurement is taken parallel to the ground, around the entire pumpkin, from blossom end to stem. These 3 measurements: over-the-top, blossom end to stem; over-the-top perpendicular to blossom end to stem and circumference, parallel to the ground at stem height, are added together and their sum is multiplied by 1.9 to give an estimate of the pumpkin's weight.

Growers who wish to contribute to the refinement of either of these two methods for estimating large pumpkin and squash weights should send the following information to the WPC.

First, estimate the weight of your pumpkin using both of these methods. Include data for over-the-top, blossom end to stem and side to side, and circumference of the fruit taken parallel to the ground at stem height. Also include the actual weight of the pumpkin taken at a weigh-off site. Send this information to the WPC, 14034 Gowanda State Road, Collins, NY 14034. This data will be used to fine tune these often used weight estimations, and help growers all over the world in determining pumpkin weights prior to actual their actual weigh-offs.

*Below: The award ceremonies are proud moments for competitive pumpkin growers. Here, Danny and Howard Dill of Windsor (left and right) flank Lanny Harbord of Port Wade, Nova Scotia Canada at the Windsor, WPC weighoff site in 1988.*

# Chapter 19 Competing With Your Pumpkin

If you grow a Dill's Atlantic Giant Pumpkin, you may as well exhibit it and compete with it in a regional weigh-off. You will get as much enjoyment from this as you got from growing the pumpkin, and you will have the opportunity to meet a lot of people that have the same interests, and enjoy the same things as you. You will soon find that there are many growers that are just as fascinated with pumpkin growing as you. In addition, a weigh-off presents a great opportunity for a family day. These special days come few and far between in today's rat race living. Many growers see weigh-off day as one of the most enjoyable family days of the year. In most cases, the weigh-off is held in conjunction with a large regional agricultural fair or craft exhibit, so the day's events hold interest for young and old. A weigh-off can bring family and friends closer together, and make life a little more enjoyable.

*Above: Ray Waterman and Ayo Ogungbuyi at the Collins, NY Pumpkin Festival and WPC Weighoff.*
*Right: Five men roll a giant pumpkin into position for a hoist into the bed of a pickup truck.*
*Below: Alan Nesbitt helps Len Stellpflug ready one of his giant squash for loading.*

Harvesting your prize winning pumpkin is not an event to take for granted. You will need the help of your family and friends, a tough tarpaulin, some strong backs and a good plan. Moving a pumpkin that weighs over 500 pounds is an awkward task. The pumpkin will be hard to get a hold of, and very, very heavy. The traditional way of lifting a giant pumpkin has been used for many years. It involves rolling the pumpkin backward to place a tarpaulin under the front end of the pumpkin, and then rolling it forward to pull the tarp to the rear. These two movements, backward and forward will allow you to position the pumpkin in the middle of the tarp, which should measure approximately 4'x4' for pumpkins up to 500 pounds, 5'x5' for 500–800 pound pumpkins and 6'x6' for pumpkins over 800 pounds. The additional size of these tarps for larger weights

allows for more people around the tarp for lifting. Tarps are available directly from the WPC, and can be purchased by writing to them.

Six people seems to be the best number to have available for the lifting, although more will not hurt. If pumpkin weights continue to go up, more people or equipment may be needed in the future. For now, with a 500 pound pumpkin, 6 people can easily loft and place it into the bed of a pickup truck. Pickup trucks seem to be the vehicles of preference by growers, although I have seen giant pumpkins transported in the back seat of a car. I do not know what is harder to do — put the pumpkin in the car, or take it out! When using a pickup truck, the pumpkin should be placed on a pallet which has been cushioned with either a heavy blanket or some other means of covering. This covering will prevent accidental damage during transport. Placing your pumpkin on a pallet allows for movement by a fork truck, if these vehicles are available at your weigh-off site. The pallet's rigid construction of wooden slats also provides for some stability against rolling or sliding during your journey to the exhibit. Make sure you position the pallet in the bed of the truck so that a fork truck can retrieve it easily. If the pallet is placed sideways, or too far forward in the bed, you will need manual assistance at the site for unloading.

*Above: Although pickup trucks are usually used for transporting giant pumpkins, occasionally you see them in the backseat of a car. Photo used courtesy of the WPC.*
*Left: Unwins Seed of the United Kingdom offered a 10,000-pound Sterling prize in 1983 to anyone in the U.K who broke the then existing world record.*
*Below: Alan Nesbitt beams with pride as he displays his winning plaques garnered from the WPC weighoff in Collins, NY.*

In most cases, plenty of help will be available at both ends of your journey. There is nothing like a giant pumpkin in attracting onlookers and enthusiastic spectators. You will probably not have much trouble either loading or unloading your pumpkin.

When trimming your pumpkin from the vine, try to leave as much of the vine as possible. Some growers believe that the more vine left, the slower the rate of water loss.

A pumpkin will begin to lose weight as soon as you trim it from the vine. Although not noticeable at first, pumpkins trimmed several days before a weigh-off or exhibit will lose weight (associated with water loss) at the rate of 1-3 pounds per day. When you are trying to squeeze as

many pounds as you can out of the growing season, it seems logical to not prematurely trim your pumpkin from the vine. The pumpkin's vine will be trimmed at the weigh-off site to a length that is consistent with the other entrants. The normal procedure is to trim the vine to within 1 inch of the pumpkin's stem.

## Rules and Regulations

Rules and regulations may vary from site to site and organization to organization, but there are some general rules followed by most weigh-offs that inject some consistency into the weighing of giant pumpkins. The WPC has done a good job in fostering guidelines which allow for some flexibility yet provides a just and fair framework in which all growers can compete. Some of the basic rules you are likely to encounter are:

An exhibitor (husband and wife as one) may enter only one specimen per class (pumpkin or squash).

An exhibitor must be present for the competition. (You cannot just drop your pumpkin off).

To be declared a pumpkin, the fruit must be cream-yellow to orange in color.

A specimen must be healthy and completely undamaged. Vines will be trimmed to one inch from stem. Foreign material may not be included in the weighing.

Weight will be rounded down to the nearest half-pound increment (example: 502.7 = 502.5 and 502.4 = 502).

The winning pumpkin will be judged by weight alone. Circumference, shape or general appearance have no bearing on the competition unless a prize sponsor has designated that their prize money goes to the most beautiful, largest in circumference, etc.

*Above: Gerry Griffin of Amston, CT poses with his 1992 pumpkin which won the "Most Uniform Dill's Atlantic Giant Pumpkin" Award at the Topsfield Fair in Topsfield, MA.*
*Below: Gary Keyzer and his family pose amongst their annual display of pumpkins. Many growers make special efforts to decorate their yards during the Halloween season, and this is enjoyed by many people in their communities.*
*Right: Joel Holland and his grandchildren enjoy all the festivities of weigh-off day. Most weigh-offs combine fairs and amusements so the day is an enjoyable event for everyone in the family.*

You may also encounter rules that exclude growers from outside your region from entering.

## After the Weigh-off

After your trip to the weigh-off, you will have to decide what to do with your giant pumpkin. Most growers simply carve them for use as giant Jack O'Lanterns, or use them for display at their homes. Growers are justifiably proud of these behemoth specimens, and showing them off seems to give as much pleasure to them as the actual growing. Growers often salvage the seed from their giant pumpkins so that they may use them for snacks or distribute them to their friends as a means of introducing others to the sport. Salvaging the seed from a particularly good pumpkin is something all growers should strive to do. There are some basic steps you should try to follow in saving seed for future years.

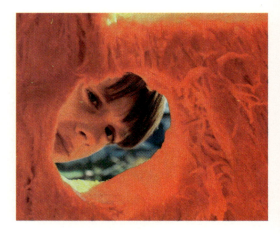

## Saving the Seed From Your Giant Pumpkin

Soon after you open and remove the seeds from within your pumpkin, you should spread them out to begin the drying process. This process will take about 3 weeks, and you should never try to expedite it by placing seed in an oven, microwave or other heating source. Drying them either indoors or outdoors is fine; however, seed left outdoors must be protected from the elements and critters. Some growers spread their seed on large screens from old doors or windows so the seed can be easily moved from place to place.

Thorough drying is the key to good storage results. Moisture will lead to decay of the seed later, especially if seed is stored in airtight containers which is highly recommended. The key is to get the moisture out, and then prevent it from returning. Three weeks of drying seems to be adequate in reducing moisture while significantly less than this puts seed in risk of later decay. After drying, the seed should be placed in air-tight containers. Mason jars, old mayonnaise jars and the like are very good containers for seed storage.

*Top: A carver peers through a hole in a giant Jack O'Lantern. Middle: Scooping the seeds from the cavity of a giant pumpkin insures treats for the kids and seed-gifts to other growers. Below: Giant pumpkins produce huge numbers of pumpkin pies.*

Storage temperatures should also be closely watched. Big fluctuations in temperature are to be avoided, and a cool, 35–50 degrees is ideal. Most unfinished basements are good places to store seed. Exposure to sunlight should also be reduced or totally eliminated. If you follow these practices, you will have good, healthy seed with high germination percentages for many years to come.

## Selling Your Giant Pumpkin

Some growers, especially regional weigh-off winners, will be approached by various people to purchase their pumpkins. Many growers are able to sell their pumpkins in the Fall to various commercial enterprises for Halloween displays. Your giant pumpkin will be quite unique in a world filled with 5–25 pound pumpkins. Restaurants, banks, car dealerships, garden centers and many other places of business see giant pumpkins as a promotional tool to increase traffic by consumers. We all know the fascination which a giant pumpkin can bring. So, you are likely to be approached by someone willing to pay for your pumpkin. Some growers

*Above: Pumpkin weighoffs are normally only part of an annual event which glorifies the role of pumpkins in our lives. Here, a large display of carving pumpkins is made available to non-growers attending the festivities.*
*Right: Growers and the family of Joel Holland pose with his world record pumpkin. The joy of setting a world record or winning a pumpkin competition is infectious, and no one is immune to it.*

even promote the sale of their giant pumpkins, and go about it in much the same way as any good businessman would. They solicit and sell to high traffic businesses every year.

Tom Cone, the Assistant Director of the NEPGA did a rough study of prices charged by growers to commercial accounts in 1992. The following guidelines are reprinted by permission of the NEPGA, and represent minimum prices for giant pumpkins.

| Weight | Price/lb. | Price |
|--------|-----------|-------|
| 100 | .30 | $30 |
| 200 | .35 | $70 |
| 300 | .40 | $120 |
| 400 | .45 | $180 |

These prices should be considered minimums, with unusually well-shaped and well-colored specimens commanding higher prices per pound. In the end, the marketplace determines the true value of your giant pumpkin. If it is big and beautiful, people will pay more for it.

# Weigh-off Sites

## World Pumpkin Confederation

### USA

**Collins, New York**
Contact: Ray Waterman, 14050 Gowanda State Road, Collins, NY 14034

**Santa Barbara, California**
Contact: Don Closson, 4144 Modoc Rd., Santa Barbara, CA 93110

**Republic, Missouri**
Contact: J.H. Cochran, 540 West Forest Lane, Republic, MO 65738

**Byron, Minnesota**
Contact: Tom Tweit, c/o Tweit's Country Fresh Market, 1821 Frontier Rd. SW, Byron, MN 55920

**Hope, Arkansas**
Contact: Wanda Hayes, Hope-Hempstead County Chamber of Commerce, Hope, AR 71801

**Oconomowoc, Wisconsin**
Contact: Jack and Pamela Marks, Marks Country Market, 5579 Marks Rd., Oconomowoc, WI 53066

**Elk Grove Village, Illinois**
Contact: Jill Stefens, Berthold Nursery and Garden Center,434 East Devon Ave., Elk Grove Village, IL 60007

**St. Johns, Michigan**
Contact: Andy and Sunday Todosciuk, c/o Andy T's Farms, 3131 S. US 27, St. Johns, MI

**Allardt, Tennessee**
Contact: George Killgore, Ag. Ext. Svc., U. of Tenn. Institute of Ag., Box 460, Jamestown, TN 38556-0460

### CANADA

**Windsor, Nova Scotia**
Contact: Danny Dill, 400 College Rd., Windsor, Nova Scotia  B0N 2T0

**Port Elgin, Ontario**
Contact: Lisa Norcross, Port Elgin Promotion Committee, Maple Square Mall, 515 Goderich St., Port Elgin, ON  N0H 2T0

**Winnipeg, Manatoba**
Contact: Kevin Twomey, T & T Seeds Ltd., Box 1710, Winnipeg, MB R3C 3P6

**Smoky Lake, Alberta**
Contact: Barry Court, Smoky Lake Pumpkin Growers Association, Box 746, Smoky Lake, Alberta  T0A 3C0

**Vancouver, British Columbia**
Contact: Christine Cheveldave, c/o Vandusen Botanical Garden, 5251 Oak St., Vancouver, BC  V6M 4H1

### UNITED KINGDOM

**Spaulding, Lincolnshire**
Contact: Bernard Lavery, 23 Hawthorn Rd., Llanharry, Pontyclun, Mid Glam., South Wales, CF7 9JD

### BELGIUM

**Duisburg**
Contact: Rene Sterckx, Huldenbergstraat, 24, B - 3080 Duisburg

### ITALY

Contact: Redento Franceschetti, c/o Club Maspiano, 25057 Sale Marasino (Brescia) Via Giardino n. 5

## New England Pumpkin Growers Association

**Topsfield, Massachusetts**
Contact: Hugh Wiberg, 445 Middlesex Ave.,Wilmington, MA 01886

## Midwestern Pumpkin Growers Association

**Anamosa, Iowa**
Contact; Tom Norlin, Rt. #2, Box 246, Hopkinton, IO 52237

## Circleville, Ohio Pumpkin Show

Contact: Circleville Pumpkin Show Committee, Circleville, OH 43113

## The Ohio Pumpkin Festival

Contact: Eugene Householder, The Ohio Pumpkin Festival, Inc., Box 5 Barnesville, OH 43713

## North West Pumpkin Growers Association

**Clackamas, Oregon**
Contact: Tallina George, c/o Tallina's Doll Supplies, 15790 S.E. Hwy. 224, Clackamas, OR 97015

## Nut Tree Art and Pumpkin Festival

**Nut Tree,California**
Contact: Mike Green, Nut Tree, Nut Tree, CA 95696

## International Pumpkin Association

**Half Moon Bay, California**
Contact: Terry Pimsleur, 2155 Union St., San Francisco, CA 94123

## Atlantic Winter Fair

Contact: David Coombs, Box 8143 Station A, Halifax, Nova Scotia, Canada  B3K 5L8

**Any pumpkin grower organizartion or pumpkin festival committee not included here should contact Don Langevin, Annedawn Publishing, P.O. Box 247, Norton, MA. Periodic revisions of this book will include additional weigh-off sites, organizations and events.**

## Seed Sources

Guerney Seed & Nursery, Yankton, SD 57079
Henry Field Seed & Nursery,Shenandoah, IA 51602
J.W. Jung Seed Co., Randolph, WI 53959
Earl May Seed & Nurserym Shenandoah, IA 51603
Burgess Seed & Plant Co., Bloomington, IL 61701
Stokes Seed Ltd., Buffalo, NY 14240
Liberty Seed Co., New Philadelphia, OH 44663
Orol Ledden & Sons, Sewell, NJ 08080
Nichols Garden Nursery, Albany OR 97321
Willhite Seed Co., Poolville,TX 76487
Zenner Bros. Seed Co., Portland, OR 97202
DeBruyn Seed Inc., Zeeland, MI 49464
Farmer Seed & Nursery, Faribault, MN 55021
Tillinghast Seed Inc., La Conner, WA 98257
Jordan Seed Inc., Woodbury, MN 55125
Rupp Seed Inc., Wauseon, OH 43567
Lockhart Seeds Inc., Stockton, CA 95201
Logan Co., Wapato. WA 98951
Leighton Seeds Inc., Salinas, CA 95201
P.L. Rohrer & Bros. Inc., Smoketown, PA 17576
Mountain Valley Seed & Nursery, Hyrum, UT 84319
Comstock, Ferre & Co., Wethersfield, CT 06109-0125
P & P Seed Co., Collins, NY 14034
Desert Cal-Seed Inc., El Centro,CA 92244-3485
Midwest Seed Growers, Lenexa, TX 66219
Bentley Seeds Inc., Buffalo, NY 14240
Harris Seeds Inc., Rochester, NY 14692-2960
R.H. Shumway's, Graniteville, SC 29829
E.S. Enterprises,Harford, MI 49057
Baxter Seed Co. Inc., Weslaco, TX 78596
Ochoa Seed Co. Inc., Gilroy,CA 95020
Weeks Seed Co., Greenville, SC 27834
Meyer Seed Co., Baltimore, MD 21231
Osborne Seed Co., Mount Vernon, WA 98273
Pennington Seeds Inc., Cullman, AL 36582
Jimmy Street Seed, Theodore, AL 36582
Ed Hume Seed, Kent, WA 98035

**A**
Acid soil 53
Alkaline soil 53
Aluminum sulfate 54
Anchor roots 106
Ants 84
Aphids 84, 87
**B**
Bacterial Wilt 87
Barber Milt 22, 79
Big Max 2-3
Bill Behuniak 60
Black, Donald 32, 38
Bone meal 77
Boron 58
Brooks, George 3
Brown, Glen 18
Bt 83, 89
Burpee's Prizewinner 3, 48
**C**
Calcium 53-54, 58, 78
Cautions 89
Chemical Fertilizers 77
Chlorophyll 58
Clackamas, Oregon 17
Cold frame 72
Competing 111
Compost 23, 57, 77, 92
Cone, Tom 28, 115
Copper 58
Cottonseed meal 77
Cover crops 58
Cucumber beetles 38, 84, 87
Cucumis 2
Cucurbita 2
    maxima 1, 6
    moschata 2
    pepo 1
        ovifera 4
Cultivation 91
**D**
Damping-Off 85
Dill, Howard 2, 11-12, 17, 20, 32, 37-38, 40, 48-49, 69, 102, 109
Dill's Atlantic Giant 2-3, 13, 17, 20, 23, 48, 67
Direct Seeding 63
Diseases 79, 81, 84, 88
    bacterial wilt 87
    damping off 85
    downy mildew 87
    gummy stem blight 85
    powdery mildew 88
    sclerotinia stem rot 85
    watermelon mosaic 87
Downy Mildew 87
Dried blood 77

**E**
Eastern States Exposition 20
Eastlund, Charles 20
Eaton, Al 42
**F**
Fertilizing 76
Field mice 93
Fisher, Karen 15
Fleming, Don 25, 33, 40, 75, 102
Flowers 96
    segments 35, 98-99
Frost 52, 62, 64, 71
Fruit Growth Stage 68-69
Fruit Setting 96
Fungicides 62, 67, 79, 89, 108
**G**
Gallagher Norm 43
Gancarz, Edward 32 38, 44
Gancarz Robert 38, 40, 44
Genuine Mammoth 13
Germination 60
Glasier Pete 17
Goderich Giant 13
Green manure 58
Greensand 77
Guinness Book of World Records 7 13 39
Gummy stem blight 79, 85
Gypsum 58
**H**
Hackney, Wayne 20, 97
Half Moon Bay 17, 116
Harvesting 111-112
Herbicides 91
Hills 59
Holland, Joel 2, 8, 32, 34, 49, 102
Holland, Matt 36
Hot bed 72
Humus 57
Hungarian Squash 2, 28
**I**
Indirect Seeding 60, 63
Insecticides 79, 89
Insects 81-82, 88
    ants 84
    aphids 84
    cucumber beetles 84
    squash bugs 83
    squash vine borers 82
Iron 58
**J**
James, John 22
**K**
Keyzer, Gary 19
Kingsbury, Al 1

**L**
Law of Limiting Factor 69-70
Leaf & Root Growth Stage 68, 78,100
Limestone 54, 58
Loading 112
**M**
MacDonald Mike 32, 37
Magnesium 58
Manganese 58
Manure 38, 51, 55, 57, 72, 76, 79, 92
McGowan, Jerry 30
Measuring 68, 109
Moles 93
Mulch 59, 92-93
Multiple fruit method 101
**N**
Nesbitt, Alan 24
NEPGA 2, 28, 115
Nitrogen 55, 77-78
Norlin, Ryan 18-19
Norlin, Tom 19
Nut Tree, 17 116
**O**
Ogungbuyi, Ayo 15, 33
Organic Fertilizer 76
Organic materials 54, 57, 59
**P**
P & P Seed Co. 15-16, 33 48 116
Peters Plantfoods 56, 77-78
PH 34, -54, 56, 58
Phosphorous 55-56, 68, 77-78
Pinching 101-102
Plant Protection 71
Plant Variety Protection 48
Planting 65
Pollen 98-99
Pollination 4, 96, 99
Potassium 55-56, 68-69, 77-78
Powdery Mildew 38, 79, 88
Pruning 36, 101
Pumpkin King 1, 8, 12, 14
Pumpkin Protection 105
**R**
Rabbits 93
Rennie Seed Co. 13
Rigoloso, Nancy and Peter 102
Ripley's Believe It or Not 7, 13
Rock phosphate 77
Rodenticide 93
Rules and Regulations 113

**S**
Sclerotinia Stem Rot 85
Screens 51
Secondary vines 75, 96
Seed Starting 60
Seed storage 114
Seedling Growth Stage 67, 69
Seedlings 61-63, 66-67, 73, 85
Selling 114
Shade and Cooling 107
Single fruit method 102
Skin cracks 106
Spacing 65
Spreader/sticker 89
Squash 1, 6, 33, 39, 59
Squash Bugs 83
Squash Vine Borers 82, 89
Squmpkin 2, 28
Stellpflug, Leonard 6, 24, 39, 109
Stem stress 36, 75, 106
Stem Stress
    shoulder stress 106
Stern's Miracle Gro 56, 77
Sulfur 89
Summer Squash 4
**T**
Tendrils 3
Testing 53, 56
Thomson, Gordon 32, 37
Topsfield Fair 2, 20, 26, 28, 38
Turk's Caps 4
**V**
Varmints 62, 93
Vine Anchoring 74
Vine Positioning 74
**W**
Wall Street Journal, The 20
Warnock, William 12, 28
Waterman Paul 15
Waterman Ray 13, 15, 33, 97
Watering 76, 79
Watermelon Mosaic 87
Weeds 91
Wiberg, Hugh 2, 28
Wind 52, 60, 64, 71
Winter squash 1, 4
Woodchucks 62, 94
Woodward, Mark 23, 73
WPC 1, 13, 15-16, 28, 38-40, 113
**Z**
Zinc 58

## Other Books Published By
## Annedawn Publishing

Annedawn Publishing is proud to make this and other books available. For information on how you can receive a copy of any of the following books, write to Annedawn Publishing, Box 247-Pumpkin, Norton, MA 02766 or ask your bookstore to order a copy for you from their book supplier.

### How-to-Grow World Class Giant Pumpkins

### Hand-Feeding Wild Birds

### The Growing and Marketing of Fall Mums